T0095233

The Cerebral Jukebox

Susan Margulies Kalish

iUniverse, Inc.
New York Bloomington

The Cerebral Jukebox

iUniverse books may be ordered through booksellers or by contacting:

iUniverse
1663 Liberty Drive
Bloomington, IN 47403
www.iuniverse.com
1-800-Authors (1-800-288-4677)

Because of the dynamic nature of the Internet, any Web addresses or links contained in this book may have changed since publication and may no longer be valid. The views expressed in this work are solely those of the author and do not necessarily reflect the views of the publisher, and the publisher hereby disclaims any responsibility for them.

ISBN: 978-1-4401-7254-0 (sc)
ISBN: 978-1-4401-7256-4 (dj)
ISBN: 978-1-4401-7255-7 (ebk)

Library of Congress Control Number: 2010902657

Printed in the United States of America

iUniverse rev. date: 5/17/2010

For my parents,
Pauline and Jack Margulies,
with gratitude

And even if you were in some prison, the walls of which let none of the sounds of the world come to your senses—would you not then still have your childhood, that precious, kingly possession, that treasure-house of memories?

~Rainer Maria Rilke

Contents

Acknowledgments

The author wishes to acknowledge the writers of the song lyrics played by *The Cerebral Jukebox*:

I Guess It Was Love
"Oh Donna": Ritchie Valens

Soldier Boy
"Soldier Boy": Luther Dixon and Florence Greenberg
"Duke of Earl": Gene Chandler, Earl Edwards, Bernie Williams
"Teenager in Love": Doc Pomus and Mort Shuman
"Blue Moon": Richard Rogers and Lorenz Hart

Let's Get It On
"Living for the City": Stevie Wonder
"Let's Get It On": Marvin Gaye

Slice of Life
"Candle in the Wind": Elton John

First Med
"Fallin'": Alicia Keyes
"Thank You": Dido

Cover photograph, 1949: ORegon-3-9833/Jack Margulies

Author photograph, back cover/Susan Margulies Kalish

Thank you to playwright Donald Margulies for permission to use the epilogue quotation.

A special thank you to my husband, Robert Kalish, for being rock-solid, dependable, and supportive.

Illustrations and Photographs

Pauline and Jack Margulies, 1943
Toys in Murray's Store Window
Bottle Caps
The Author with Her Mother
The Vase
Stuyvesant Town
The Author with Her Sister
Florida, 1966
Shepard Hall, C.C.N.Y.
The Orvieto Cathedral
Birthing at Bocuse
Who Have Become Crows
Moon Maggot
Grandmother, Sophie Kolsadt
The Bog Man
Article in the *New York Times*, August 8, 1936
Suzanne Loew
The Observer
The Cricket Convention
Couples
The Flatiron Building
Soul Food
Slice of Life
Dragonfly
Lamentation
Playground 5; the Author with Her Father

Toys in Murray's Store Window, 1949
Photograph/Jack Margulies

Introduction

This is a collection of urban poems—or maybe poems of an urban mind. Someone called me an "accessible writer," and that's probably true. I want to take the reader with me on my journeys. Largely autobiographical and confessional, or founded on observation and reaction, most of my poems were written during 2001 and 2002, when I took a sabbatical from teaching so I could return to writing and art. It was the year that my city, as I knew it, came apart. The collection has been augmented in recent years on my blog, The Cerebral Jukebox.

I was born in New York City and have lived here all my life. I was raised in Stuyvesant Town, a middle-class housing development on the Lower East Side of Manhattan. Right after World War II, at a time when there was a severe housing shortage, many veterans were able to find affordable housing in this new, eighty-acre apartment complex, built where aging tenements once stood. For better or worse, these one hundred look-alike pink buildings molded me. The uniformity was bland, yet comforting; I was one of many children lucky enough to grow up in this midcity haven.

In the first grade, I began writing my own lyrics to television show theme songs: *Kukla, Fran and Ollie*, *The Howdy Doody Show*, *Rootie Kazootie*. I collected the prizes in cereal boxes and mailed away for special offers touted on the backs of comic books. I always wanted a piano but never got one, so I sang and accompanied myself on my mother's egg slicer. I watched Queen Elizabeth's coronation on a small black-and-white television screen—while suffering from the worst stomach virus on earth.

My childhood spirit was fed by Orange Humorettes, fifteen-cent pizza slices, greasy square knishes from Koburn's Deli, and penny candy. I played with yo-yos, tops, dolls, and hula hoops. My shelves were filled with board games; Monopoly and Candy Land were favorites. I occupied myself drawing chalk games on sidewalks. I made skully caps from the bottle tops of Myer 1890 Ginger Ale or Mott's Prune Juice, filling the caps with melted Crayola Crayons. My world was shaped by the Tompkins Square Branch of the New York Public Library, subways (which were often elevated), Dick Clark, pop music, and anything else in the collective memory of the baby boomer age of innocence.

The Cerebral Jukebox is the player that reflects my memories on gray-matter disks.

Mine never stops playing.

Susan Margulies Kalish
New York City
2010

Part 1
Innocence

Dedicated to my sister, Laura

The author with her mother, Pauline Margulies
Stuyvesant Town, New York City, 1949
Photograph/Jack Margulies

The innocent and the beautiful have no enemy but time.
~William Butler Yeats

1

Illustration/Susan Margulies Kalish

The Vase

The apartment was filled
with antique Chinese embroideries in silk
on the walls:
huge birds with long feathers, peonies, trees
painted with long stitches in blues and greens and pinks.
Framed in mahogany.
Ginger jars turned into lamps
reflected the color scheme, as did
the upholstery of the furniture and the carpet.
Between the dining room and the living room
stood a tall, black bookcase,
standing guard, wearing
my mother's beloved
Ming vase like a crown.
High atop the shelves,
safe from catastrophe,
it sat regally, viewing the room
until the little child threw her panda,
black and white,
into the air, wheeee!
high into the air
until it met the vase and
sent it
crashing
to
the
floor.

I saw the descent, so slow yet so quick
I saw it, I heard it, I watched as it
hit the floor and broke apart,
the black floral vase
into so many pieces,
so many little fragments.

How does something whole break apart?
How does a child start whole,
and, so slowly yet so quickly,
fall prey to time,
and break apart
in black and white
like a panda bear?

Yellow Butterfly Dress

That butterfly was the last one.
Butterflies don't live in here, in the ghetto.
~ Pavel Friedman

Dedicated to Pavel Friedman, who was born in Prague on January 7, 1921, and deported to the Terezin Concentration Camp on April 26, 1942. He died in Auschwitz on September 29, 1944.

My sister was born in December.
I was six years old. And by the summer
when our 1950s apartment was stifling and my
father was weary from work and heat,
my mother sent him on vacation
to the Catskill Mountains. It didn't matter that *she*
needed a rest from an infant
and a soon-to-be second-grader.
She sent my dad.
He took me with him.

We went to a place far from the city,
where the blaze of summer bounced
off the lake and hit the tree tops;
The Pine Tree Country Club,
a small, run-down hotel,
composed of a gaggle of little bungalows,
each with a sagging wooden, cracked-paint porch,
and its very own wasps' nest glued under the eaves.
There was also an old casino.

Each pair of bungalow couples shared a bathroom.
There was an old black-and-white television in the casino
and movies were projected on a screen at night.

My father got me a T-shirt; it was white and had
the emblem of a pine tree, raised in faux, dark green velvet
and the words *Pine Tree Country Club.*
It was itchy as all hell.

I had bad allergies:
Each morning my father opened a fragile clear capsule
and spilled teeny little pink and white pills into a spoon
and then onto my tongue.

We sat by the lake in Adirondack chairs that had probably been there
as long as the hotel—from the twenties or thirties.
Perhaps this had once been
a classy retreat for wealthy city dwellers.
But now the working class was here,
sitting by the lake, for a week or two;
then it was back to reality.

My father was a laborer; he packed and lifted huge boxes of
raincoats and shipped them for the Neptune Raincoat Company
on the Lower East Side of Manhattan, grunting in the heat in
his undershirt in a warehouse.
But here, by the lake, he was king in his untucked tropical shirt
with the large green leaf pattern.

The lady next door tried in vain to braid my hair to my specifications,
and I protested to my father who shushed me as
we slammed the door of the bungalow. We woke the wasps
who were angered and swarmed over my father;
one managed to get a good bite of his bald head.
My father didn't want to show me he was in pain, but
I sensed it. Someone told him to *put mud on it.*
We went to the lake where the previous day he hid a
garter snake in his tropical shirt pocket and it peed
a yellow puddle of fear. This time it was my father's turn to be
scared, but I helped him by putting a mud pie on his head.

During our week at the lake,
I learned how to play "Chopsticks" on the tinny old casino piano.
I climbed up on a huge, cracked red leather-topped bar stool
and asked the bartender for a ginger ale.
I sat on the toilet and watched Cookie, my pet fly,
crawl up my arm.
It was the country,
this was my version of nature.

One morning, I put on my yellow sundress and after breakfast
we went to the lake. The sun was bright,
the sky intensely blue and cloudless,
minnows bubbled to the top of the murky green water.
I sat in the large lake chair, my legs straight out, and watched
one, two, three, seven, eleven yellow butterflies
flutter onto my dress and latch on; fifteen, twenty-two; my
dress was calling to them, like guiding them to a runway
at an airport; thirty-four, thirty-five …
I was covered in butterflies; small, silky, stubborn, baby-skinned
little creatures that refused to let go when I tried to brush them off
with shrieks and jumps and shakes.
I was terrified.
I never knew the intensity
of such intimacy before.

I was so lucky.

Stuyvesant Town under construction
View from 653 East 14th Street, 1947
Photograph/Jack Margulies

Black and White

His Graflex, Rollei, Canon, Leica
were his voice; he didn't speak,
but he recorded his poetry
on film, writing with light,
on endless rolls
of silver-coated, sprocketed curls
that he would load into his cameras
and *shoot.*

When the number in the little window, or on
the turning metal indicator reached twenty-four
or sometimes thirty-six,
he would rewind the film and remove it
from a trap door.
Then we would go into the closet
where it was black, and silent,
between the coats,
so quiet you could hear
the blood rushing through your ears,
except when he was loading the film
into the developing canister;
swoosh, swoosh, swoosh.

The Kodak man stayed securely
in my hand, glowing in the dark, greenish,
a plastic profile of a cartoonish man
in a 1950s hat, like a news reporter,
holding a camera, like my father's.
Maybe the Kodak man was meant to swing on a
chain to turn a red safety light on and off,
but he was mine.

In the kitchen the film was loaded, developed,
bathed, and unwound.

He put the strips into the enlarger
that sat next to the broiler
and cooked up images of
the Lower East Side;
buildings, people, interactions,
then burned them with light
onto the paper,
and bathed them in a vinegary pond
in a pan in
the kitchen sink.
Up came the images, darker and clearer:
the faces, the streets, the tenements,
the sky, the people sitting near the
East River.
The family. Me.
Preserved happy moments
of light-jelly in paper jars.
The poetry of his Graflex,
calling for future stanzas to be written
by a then
Kodak Brownie.

1959

1

Good Humor

The Stuyvesant Town trees are heavy with green,
and Fernando, the Good Humor man
with the gray-white hair and mustache,
claims his post on the corner of
Fourteenth Street and Avenue B.
He holds court on a blue milk crate throne,
next to his little white cart
with the scratched metal top
that I'd tap with my coins.
I give him fifteen cents for an Orange Humorette
and he says, "Here, Tottalina."
He opens the thick door with the heavy latch
and digs down, with his red hands,
into the smoky, cold, icy depths
and retrieves my white, paper-wrapped prize.
He gives it to me
along with the three cents change
he has clicked out of the
coin sorter on his belt.

The first lick is frigid and tasteless,
too cold to sense.
It sticks to my tongue, teasing me,
then warms,
becoming the familiar exotic orange,
yielding to vanilla within.

I know both pleasure and pain.
It's like I have gotten to the top of a mountain
and now it is time for the descent;
soon I will be at the bottom,
and I will be licking
the stick
to splinters.

2

Potsy

Pre-puberty,
scraped knees,
Barbie doll.
Life's boundaries are defined by chalk lines
on the pavement near the playground.
A light breeze blows through my hair.
There is comfort in ritual
and joy in being.
At the potsy court, drawn in pink, tenuous lines,
I am throwing my skate key,
or a pebble or an ice cream stick into the boxes,
and then I dance my solo
hopscotch waltz
from box to box,
hopping, skipping, jumping,
dipping to retrieve the key,
spinning and reversing,
back I come,
my hair
flying.

3

Planes

Then, I stop.
An airplane!
My mind sings the song I copied
into a composition book, with large letters,
and memorized:
Oh the aer-o-plane, oh the aer-o-plane,
Can go faster than the fastest train,
Faster than the ships at sea,
'Cause it flies right through the air you see.
Up so high, up so high!
How we love to watch it fly.

I stand, shielding my eyes from the sun
in a salute.
I have become a face,
turned upward,
my sticky mouth ajar,
in wonder of how
the sky could be *that* blue,
and how a plane could be *that* huge,
and *that* silver,
and low-flying,
and loud,
with its four droning propellers.
Not like the sound of future jets,
with their deep, low roar that vibrates in your gut.
No,
this was a lulling signal, from another place.
My planes hung in the sky,
gleaming behemoths above my head,
and as they passed,

in slow motion,
I secretly prayed
and played the game:
Will it, can it, stay up?
Why, of course it can!

Pan American, or TWA,
going far, far away.
Maybe even to Florida!

4

Propellers

So many times and years later
when I have been unable to surrender to rest,
I yielded to the silence and quieted my heart
to listen for the drone of my propeller planes.
They come from deep within the clouds,
taking those lucky people to Florida,
who look down at me
and see the speck
of my upturned, now adult face, in the moonlight.
As they eat their peanuts
and watch Doris Day,
they smile, dreaming of palm trees and oranges,
while ensconced, aloft
in their silver shell.
Finally, I can hear the lullaby
of the engines;
I peel open my Orange Humorette,
toss my skate key into the pink chalk box,
and safe at last,
in 1959,
I fall asleep.

Credo

How wonderful it is that nobody need wait a single moment before
starting to improve the world.
~Anne Frank

The early 1960s

1

Lord have mercy upon us.

This I know is true:
Kyrie eleison.
The Church of
the Immaculate Conception
on East Fourteenth Street,
held a soiled, once-white marble Madonna
in a niche
on its black, polluted façade.
On Sundays, the bells rang at 9:00 AM.
Maybe earlier.
The nuns walked along the street in pairs
toward First Avenue,
in their hawk-wing black habits,
their crosses long and heavy,
swinging from their necks.

2

Glory be to God on high
and on Earth, peace to men of good will.

This I know is true:
Gloria in excelsis Deo.
Et in terra pax
Hominibus bonae voluntatis.
At 3:00 PM on school days,
children in blue insignia-ed uniforms
spilled from the doors
with untamed energy, pent up,
rebellious from the fear of a ruler across their knuckles.
Murderer!
You killed Jesus!

3

We praise Thee. We bless Thee.
We worship Thee. We glorify Thee.

This I know is true:
Laudamus te, benedicimus te,
Adoramus te, glorificamus te.
The shame.
There is no one to confess to:
Jews do not confess.
They internalize guilt.
Murderer, Jew Bastard!
I am an eight-year-old killer.

4

Thou that takest away the sins of the world, have mercy on us.
Thou that takest away the sins of the world, receive our prayer.

This I know is true:
Qui tollis peccata mundi, miserere nobis.
Qui tollis peccata mundi, sucipe deprecationem nostram.
I see Rabbi Sidney shuffling along
by the playground;
he is coming home from temple.
The sun follows him.
He is tall and slightly bent. Rigid and slow moving,
as though the bones of his body have been fused
by a heavy weight.
His nose is the foundation
for the large, heavy glasses
that magnify his foggy irises and the lines on his cheeks.
His ears are as big as the handles on Russel Wright sugar bowls;
they have heard everything.
I speed to him, calling his name.
He turns around slowly.
He looks down at me.
Old man white stuff has collected
at the corners of his lips
and seals them against my question.
"Rabbi Sidney,
why do they call me dirty Jew?"

5

I believe in one God,
The Father Almighty,
Maker of heaven and earth,
And of all things visible and invisible.

This I know is true:
Credo in unum Deum,
Patrem omnipotentem,
Factorem coeli et terrae,
Visibilium omnium et invisibilium.
Victoria Elizabeth Smith,
my best friend,
and I
are playing skully;
we speed bottle caps filled with melted Crayolas
from box to numbered box.
I have gone to
St. George's Church with her
to hear E. Power Biggs
play the magnificent organ.
There go the caps.
And here comes the battle.
Dirty Jews!
The world is full of us, it seems.
We are dirty Jews and dirty *Episcopal* Jews;
Everyone is a dirty Jew who doesn't wear *The Imac* uniform.
My mother calls
Father McCabe on the black extension phone in the bedroom
and says,
"Why don't you teach tolerance?"
She slams down the receiver.

6

Blessed is he that cometh
in the name of the Lord.
Hosanna in the highest.

This I know is true:
Benedictus
Qui venit in nomine Domini.
Osanna in excelsis.
I am walking with Susan Greene,
her dad trailing behind us;
we pass a forbidden playground.
The gates open and the onslaught is upon us.
We are surrounded.
I fought.
She fled.

I looked to her father, the adult, the protector,
but his face was white-quiet,
watching me through the barbed wire of
his Auschwitz.

7

Oh Lamb of God,
That taketh away the sins of the world:
Have mercy upon us.
Grant us peace.

Agnus Dei,
Qui tollis peccata mundi,
Miserere nobis.
Dona nobis pacem.

This I know is true.

I Guess It Was Love

I am wearing the shirtwaist my mother made
on her new Singer sewing machine.
She loved that machine; she'd pop in special discs
to make embroidery.

I still hear her singing arias from *Kismet*
while sitting and stitching
turquoise rows around the skirt of my new yellow dress.

I was in the sixth grade at P.S. 61.
It was 1959, and I was leaving the
cocoon of elementary school the following year
headed for departmentalized classes,
about to tote lunch bags.
(I had always gone home for lunch.)
The world was about to change. Radically.
A school dance. For sixth-graders.

I wore the yellow dress
and kids called me "Lemon Drop."
Richie Valens's "Oh Donna" is amplified
and overly loud and distorted,
bouncing from one wall to another
in the huge room where
we played volleyball. The gym.
Painted lines
on the floor, dividing us,
literally, into the bullies and the bullied,
the sullied, the elite, the despised, the popular, the loners.
We were all there, ready to be launched like rockets
into adolescence.

Sheldon Panik is walking toward me. I *am* panicked.
He always looked older, smelled older. His hair flops over his

eyes in strands greased like Elvis Presley's. It's black, his eyes are
coal-like, sultry; his bottom lip is sensual; he licks it.
I am overcome by fear.

Oh Donna, Oh Donna.
Oh God. I begin to shrink.

I watched *American Bandstand* every afternoon at 4:00 PM.
I could do the bop, the fox-trot
(learned by standing on my father's feet),
the cha-cha, the mambo.
I longed to be one of those TV teenagers, dancing and flirting,
looking happy, perfect, in saddle shoes.
Dick Clark never warned me about Panik.
Sheldon panic.
He looked *huge*.
I was probably five feet tall. He must have been five feet four.
He wore one of those shirts that was semi-dressy and not tucked in,
with a longitudinal pattern running down the front
on both sides of the buttons.
Must have gotten it from his older brother.
I am starting to sweat in my lemon drop dress.
He extends his hand.
He is smiling.
I am eleven.
I take it.
I become a wooden plank.

Oh Donna ...

We are doing a slow two-step, near the wall.
I can't control myself and start to laugh.
It's the laugh of a hysteric.
The laugh of a kid in class who finds something *so* inane that
the giggles grow geometrically.
It's the laugh of someone trying harder than *anything*
to *stop* laughing.
And can't.

If I'd been drinking milk,
it would have come out my nose.

We sway. I am a two by four. Grinning, trying to be adult.
Ready to burst.
He is wearing cologne.
There is a musky odor behind it, an odor I don't recognize.
It is June. It is hot. Heat changes everything.
It is a catalyst of emergence
for flowers, fragrances, freshness, color, action.
It was new. I was giddy.
I couldn't catch my breath;
my face was frozen in a hot, manic smile.
Maybe *this* was love?

Donna, where can you be?
Where can you be?

Sheldon lived on the poor side
of East Fourteenth Street, in a tenement.
I lived across the street,
in a huge, middle-class housing development
where thousands and thousands
of windows reflected windows.

A friend told me
that early one Saturday morning
Sheldon stood in front of a building near mine
and for hours called my name,
until he got hoarse and
went home.

Donna where can you be?
Where can you be?

I guess it was love.

Soldier Boy

It was small enough to fit in my hand,
the transistor radio, ready with fresh batteries.
I got it in 1960, when I graduated from P.S. 61.
My dad brought it home.
It was red, in a brown leather case
with a cutout on the side for the knob.
The stick-marker tread from left to right
across the AM numbers,
searching for songs.

When the nights were heavy with heat,
we'd flee our apartments.
Our faces were red from the beach,
yet we'd be shivering from the burn.
We'd pull on our stretch denims
and nylon Windbreakers that went
over our heads and covered our hips. Zipped at the top.
White or pink or baby blue. Pocket in the front.

Sometimes I'd pick up Shelly;
we'd tease our hair in front of her mirror and
insert small bows on clips between our bangs and
the poof of the *bouffant flip*.
I was twelve? Thirteen?
Amazed that my brown hair had
gold threads of blond woven throughout.
And no one had green eyes like me.
She'd put on the Shirelles:
Soldier boy,
Oh, my little soldier boy
I'll be true to you.
The guitar would twang. We'd sing.
Then it was time to go.
Teenagers came down hundreds of elevators

from all over Stuyvesant Town,
walking in pairs, in groups,
joyful, excited.
To the northwest corner
of Playground Ten, outside the fence;
its gate was locked shut, religiously,
at the prescribed time.
Now it was empty.
But when the sun was bright, little kids
loved to zip down the ramp at the entrance
on their metal trikes.

Lit by street lamps,
a hundred or more of us would keep
a multitude of families awake past 10:00 PM.
Their windows, gaping to catch air,
allowed our uninvited din in,
while fans inside the hot apartments
recirculated heat.

We bombarded them with our teenage laughter:
the chasing, tagging, squealing.
The tripping over cobblestones,
the climbing on benches.
The gawking, flirting, clusters of faces
under acne cream.
We were drowning in our hormonal soup,
too old to play jump rope, too young to date.

There was one thing no one could touch or banish:
Our radio waves.

Today, fingers fly over BlackBerrys;
small phone pads send text messages.
But we, *we* were empowered by our
prehensile thumbs, our agile index fingers
that turned radio dials in unison when the command made

its way through the troops:
880—CBS! Duke of Earl!

As the message passed through us,
a hundred or more radios locked onto
the signal and created the most magnificent stereo:
Duke, Duke, Duke, Duke of Earl ...
Duke, Duke of Earl ...

Mothers glared from open windows,
holding wailing infants;
pre-teens peered out from behind curtains, envious.
Fathers in undershirts
wondered how
they would get up for work.

We were like aliens on another planet,
with our own language.
Each evening, Stuyvesant Town security guards
warned us, then gave up;
we couldn't understand them in our giddiness.

WMGM! Dion and the Belmonts!
Why must I be a teenager in love?

Then the hunger:
for ice cream, for love.
We painted our nails in *Revlon Frosted Bamboo White,*
coated our lips in *Waikiki Pink,*
and ate fifteen-cent slices of pizza.

Blue moon, you saw me standing alone,
Without a dream in my heart ...

We walked lockstep into adolescence
over hot sand at Jones Beach,
through more school years,

carrying heavier books,
holding the hand
of a first love—
until the world could no longer fit
in our palms.

We walked into adolescence.
All the way to the Vietnam War.

The author and her sister, Laura Margulies
Brighton Beach, Brooklyn, New York, 1958
Photograph/Jack Margulies

Birthday Doll

I might have been twelve, so
you were six and under my care;
Mom worked.
She brought home the groceries after a day
at the Dictaphone machine and
the ninety words per minute
typewriter,
stepped out of her high heels,
returning to five feet tall.

She handed me five dollars and told me
to take you to buy a birthday present.
"OK, Ma," I think I dutifully answered.

She must have been tired, really tired,
to have forgotten to pick up a gift
and to send us out in the dark.

I suppose she was going to start making dinner.
Sometimes, after we ate,
she'd clear the little kitchen counters
and set up the typewriter,
the old Remington.
She would sit on the thick Manhattan Yellow Pages,
atop the step stool, typing briefs for the
law firm on the corner, and invoices
for dad's camera repair business—his second job.
I don't know how such a little woman
could work so much
and still take care of a family.

It was a December evening,
around five o'clock,
a Wednesday.

We put on our jackets,
took the elevator down;
it was dark and cold,
my stomach was quaking.
I held your hand
and clutched the five-dollar bill.

We walked ten minutes or more,
under the lamplights,
around the playground,
down the wide stairs
onto Fourteenth Street, Avenue B,
then to Avenue A.
A bus lumbered along Fourteenth Street,
coming from Union Square,
bringing people home from the subway,
and shoppers from S. Klein's—
the best bargain department store around.

If I were to walk those city blocks today,
I know they would seem shorter and
possibly more interesting;
but then, the streets seemed endless,
and in the darkness they took on an aura
that was familiar yet distorted by neon.

Our side, the Stuyvesant Town side,
was lined with pink building after pink building,
each eleven stories,
now grayish in the diminished light.
Across Fourteenth Street, the stores were lit
and beckoned brightly like a circus:
The Prince of Pizza on the corner,
where I would have my first slice and burn my mouth;
Town Rose Bakery,
where the lady with black hair and long red nails
stuffed pastry into boxes and tied them up with red and white string;

the little law office, where Mom sometimes worked;
Woolworth's,
where we bought our pet GiGi, the Java Temple bird;
PermaCut,
where we sat in airplane seats in the basement and Mr. Joseph cut our hair;
John's Bargain Store,
where we'd pick through bins of vinyl and plastic;
Thom McCann Shoes, where I would later get the first pair of little heels
that I wore to Paul Leonard's bar mitzvah;
Barricini Chocolates,
on the corner of Avenue A, where the smell of cocoa was overwhelming;
Pam Pam Burgers, juicy, with the shiny, puffy bun,
and maybe twenty more stores in between.

It was nice to feel your hand in mine;
I was so adult and in control,
a small mother. My ears rang with cold, under my hat.
You were probably in kindergarten,
no longer a four-year-old with a
baby tummy, full and rounded from your chest down.
Still small and fragile, with large blue eyes and ash hair,
you ran to keep up with me.

We arrived at the corner of Fourteenth Street and First Avenue,
where the subway was,
the LL line to Brooklyn that we knew went to
our two grandmas and to the beach.
Traffic picked up here, yellow taxis honking their way
uptown on First Avenue;
we turned right at the corner.

There were shops embedded into the First Avenue side
of our cookie-cutter buildings;
a Kodak store,
where Dad's photo of me and another little girl
was blown up into a poster and once displayed;
a Good Humor store—or did that come later?

An original Howard Johnson's restaurant that
later became something with an Irish name.
McKenna's?
The First National City Bank,
its name on a highly polished brass medallion.
Banking hours: 9:00 AM to 3:00 PM

And then! There! Next door!
Murray's!
Toys!
(My dad once took a picture of tiny me
pointing at the toys in the window.)
Toys to the right.
Housewares, pots, curtains, measuring cups,
appliances, to the left.

When we entered the store,
we left the darkness and chill behind,
and fluorescent lights took over.
Metal trucks, cars, bubble blowers, things to build, puzzles,
games in long rectangular boxes,
coloring books—they all beckoned.
Then we found the dolls.

You pointed to a baby doll
in a cardboard box,
looking out through the cellophane window.
I see myself reaching for it, pulling it down,
handing it to you;
and in my pre-teen awkwardness,
I asked in an overly loud, take-charge,
impatient parent voice:
"Is *this* the one you want?"
You liked the blue dress and
the glass eyes that opened and closed.
I handed the man the money.
He put the box in a bag and

gave me change.

We went out onto the dark, busy street;
it felt like midnight, and I wasn't ready
for the burden of responsibility.
I silently questioned why
it was given to me.

We walked back the way we came,
the neon now on our right,
the wind pushing us along
to lamb chops, or meat loaf, or chicken.

I can still feel your hand in my hand.

The Cerebral Jukebox

Victoria Elizabeth, named after her mother,
lived in an apartment on the top floor of an eleven-story tower
overlooking the Lower East Side of Manhattan.
From her living-room window
she could see to the horizon,
to where the Brooklyn and Manhattan bridges
formed necklaces.

Her nickname was *Ping*.

I live in that apartment
in my memory;
mind-music of
nineteen fifties and sixties.

We were two little girls in elementary school.
Standing at her window,
she is still next to me.
Victoria, with her blond pixie haircut,
her blue eyes framed in
orange harlequin eyeglasses
locked to her face by a ski jump nose.
My little friend,
Ping,
who shared a bedroom with her parents
in a three-room apartment.

The floors were parquet wood, uncovered,
against Stuyvesant Town regulations:
Carpet, on eighty percent of the floor.
But no one below seemed to complain when we clacked about
like dancers in our Thom McCann flats or little heels,
tapping like adults.
Oh, I loved the sound, the feel of my shoes

striking the floor.

I went home to green carpets and art on the walls.
To chinoiserie, lit lamps, wing chairs. A menorah.
To suppers, served reliably at 6:00 PM.
Ping's youthful blond aunt came over to pick her up one evening;
she sat in the lady chair, looked around and said,
"It's so lovely here."

But at Ping's house
the rooms were spare,
a canvas butterfly chair here,
a couch there,
a black-and-white television
with splayed rabbit ears.

One Sunday morning, her father started up
the turntable with Josh White,
followed by Judy Collins,
then Odetta.
He showed me the record jackets;
I smelled liquor on his breath.
He had been through World War II;
he woke during the nights screaming,
his face wet and reddened by
Japan.
I was once there when her mother fell asleep on the couch;
drink took her to sleep,
where she spoke in the foreign tongues
of dreams.

Ping wore the key to her apartment around her neck
on a graying piece of string.
It dangled between her dress and undershirt.
While in junior high school, while her mother was at work,
she brought a boy home from the other side of the tracks,
maybe from Second Avenue?

They were making out on the couch,
and the wires of their braces got interlocked;
the scene a far cry from the days in sixth grade
when we made prank phone calls
from the greasy, black, kitchen wall phone,
laughing until we cried, hanging up the
receiver without guilt.

High school separated us;
she traveled uptown to hers,
I traveled downtown to mine,
within the purview of her windows,
a school embedded in an area
where immigrants once bought from
rows of pushcarts
and fished in pickle barrels.
The last time I saw her,
she wore knee-high black leather boots.
We sat on my bed and did geometry.

Years later, I met Lucy, a mutual friend,
in a ladies' room at C.C.N.Y.
I asked about Ping.
Her father had passed away:
Fell in the street
or something.
Ping.
Was it she who came home for Christmas, or spring break,
to find her mother dead
on the kitchen floor?
Days' worth of death from
malnutrition.
Or something.

I listened to red-headed Lucy in the room with
frosted glass. Water running.
Toilets flushing. I saw her mouth moving.

I heard the words.
I was nineteen years old.
If I was holding something, I dropped it.
If I could have understood what I was hearing, I would have.
If I had seen my face in a mirror at that moment,
I would not have known who I was.

I often think of the view from Ping's apartment.
The world was small but vast.
Looking out, I could focus on the tenements,
their sad faded brown façades, the stoops,
the small uneven shops:
Koburn's Deli,
Freidel's Luncheonette,
Weissman's Children's Clothes,
China Boy Restaurant.
There, the red and white-faced Carvel.
I feel the weight of a frosty Brown Bonnet
in my hand, the swirled vanilla custard cone
dipped in chocolate and frozen.

Look! Further down. Tompkins Square Park.
And the library on East Tenth Street,
once grand.
I see rickety metal cellar covers
embedded in the sidewalks;
they clanged when people walked on them.
The sagging storefront
where Mr. Brandt cobbled
broken shoes,
his eyes darting over his glasses
to the action in the street,
a girly calendar with a Cat's Paw ad
behind him on the peeling wall lined with shoes.
His shop smelled of old, cracked, dirty leather,
machine oil, and cigars;
Auschwitz was blue-tooled into his arm.

I can see the beginning of the Puerto Rican influx:
I watch the little Spanish girls treading carefully
on icy winter streets,
to P.S. 61 on
East Twelfth Street and Avenue B,
in thin yellow or pink nylon ruffled
party dresses with black sashes,
little white anklet socks in black Mary Janes.
Shivering in sweaters,
their curls bouncing as they ran,
little girls who left the Caribbean
and who ate the school lunch of
peanut butter and jelly on whole wheat;
with tomato soup.

I can still smell the soup.

I could see all the way down
to Canal Street, or so I thought,
where my father worked for years at
the Neptune Raincoat Company,
laboring and loading in his torn T-shirt, until his face was red
and his hairy back was wet.

I could see and remember all of this,
all that I saw and thought I saw,
all that I knew and thought I knew.
From that living room window,
I looked down and out and up and
through gold and pink-swept skies,
after school on spring days,
to bridges and to pigeons flying in formation over rooftops,
over greening treetops,
to the East River and to gliding tugboats.
I still see the round water towers
with pointy hats,
perched atop the aging buildings,

on skinny stilts,
like a gaggle of long-limbed water fowl.

If I were to look up,
so many years later,
I might not be able to see where I once stood.
I'd have to crane my head back to
find the window, among hundreds, searching,
squinting, and pointing to hold my place,
blinded by reflections and the glare of time passing.
And if I *could* find it, *if I could get to it*,
if I could touch the old glass in that living room,
the fingerprint fog of childhood would prevent me
from recognizing the world I knew.
But the view will forever remain,
to play and play again.

In my Cerebral Jukebox.

Part 2
Conflicts

Florida, 1966
Photograph/Susan Margulies Kalish

Change alone is eternal, perpetual, immortal.
~Arthur Schopenhauer

Civil War

1

It was 1966,
in the heat of an eighteen-thousand-BTU summer,
after running away from home to Florida
at age seventeen,
on a two-week lam.
Told my parents they were *stupid,*
and *seventeen years too late.*
I was wedged between Seward Park High School,
C.C.N.Y.,
and raging hormones,
in a rented car
next to the eighteen-year-old man I would
eventually marry,
though both too young.
Eating in diners with
signs on the walls:
We reserve the right to deny service
to blacks and Jews.

The Formica was greased by pork,
the waitress was southern fat,
her face young and round,
she lisped when reciting
the names of pies,
so pecan pies
sounded like *pecan p-eye-th.*
And there were key lime pies,
and fear,
because we *were* Jews.

The billboards reflected the
Civil War:

Even Yankees Like Southern Bread,
I'd Even Go North for Southern Bread.
On to Daytona Beach,
where I was
too young to buy cigarettes,
but not too young
for the cheap motel rooms.
Or the need,
or the hunger,
for love,
for lust, or
for burgers at 2:00 AM.

2

His parents were away,
on the heat-heavy night of our return
on Eastern Airlines:
Number one to the sun.
And we were driven
to the frigid refuge of
his parents' bedroom.

Then, with
partially unpacked bags,
commingled damp underwear,
condoms,
Kools,
cold, white, king-size sheets,
our skin tannned,
wearing our hair
and our watches,
we slept entwined
until the light crept
through the venetian blinds
and painted slats on our faces.

3

But then!
The sound of a key in the door,
and the scraping of metal,
and the heavy screech of
the police lock wedged into the floor,
but coming free.

It was Aunt Selma,
checking up on her nephew!
Aunt Selma,
who left Uncle Nathan behind
while she performed this mitzvah
for her sister Greta.
Aunt Selma,
all five feet of her,
her white hair,
her eyes magnified behind her thick glasses:
"Ach! Steven, vere are yoo?"

She began to push through the old
glass double doors to the bedroom
while he screamed,
"Aunt Selma! Don't come in!"
And I dove for the floor,
piling covers over me,
playing *lump*,
my heart pounding against
my naked chest.
"Everything's OK, Aunt Selma,
Everything's OK!"

But she wouldn't budge:
she stood eagle-eyed
at the foot of the bed,
which had obviously been made good use of

and covered with
prima facie evidence.

She took it all in and
prepared to issue a report
upon her sister's return:
the bra, the panties,
the Kools, the condom wrappers,
the now-bare pillows with two head imprints,
the venetian blind slats.
But she never found me,
tan and terrified,
playing *lump*,
shivering on the floor.

Let's Get It On

I am in our 1969 Grand Prix;
Steve is driving.
We are in our mid-twenties;
it is the summer of
1974, and this night is hot;
we have left the Bronx
and our destination
is the Upper West Side of Manhattan.
We are going to a party.
I know no one.

Steve is six feet tall, blond, in good shape.
Long hair, probably a mustache,
that's what men had in those days;
they were influenced
by record album covers,
by the likes of Crosby, Stills, Nash & Young.
He was probably wearing his brown Frye boots,
tight, boot-cut jeans, and a sort of western shirt
with pearl snaps, one that hugged his lean body.

I don't have a clear picture of myself;
I was still forming,
still observing the world
from behind a mask, insecure.
But I knew this: my hair was dark and long, and my eyes,
as they are now,
were masters of inner movie making,
always taking notes, always soaking up
the nuances of people
and the events around them.

We parked
a few blocks away

from an old apartment building,
once majestic.
In the early '70s, in the summer heat,
the streets were always littered,
the city steamed rotting garbage,
it reeked of dog and human piss. But
nothing really mattered
when you were young,
or high.

Life wasn't a threat, it was an adventure,
as was the adventure of being self-absorbed.
We entered the small hot apartment, where
box fans blew the air around and
furniture looked old and impermanent.
I remember people laughing, talking.
Bowls of potato chips, probably dips, cheese, maybe cake—
possibly even Alice B. Toklas brownies, paper cups,
7-Up, Coke, Pink Catawba,
and Mateus in its flat, round bottle.
The usual.

I remember the sounds of
Stevie Wonder, Marvin Gaye,
and the smell of smoke.
There was a record player against the wall,
and it was swallowing vinyl discs on a spindle.
There were young women in colorful Indian skirts, long,
rich, and flowing. Peasant blouses, dangly earrings.
Women dancing with women; mirror images, bright sandaled feet,
skirt into skirt, knees into knees. Men grooving.

Livin' just enough for the city ...

I was very much alone at this party,
a voyeur, while
Steve did his usual; he smoked his brains to a pulp.

Bubbling smoke through his water pipe.
His blue eyes popped bloodshot red.
He *munchied* his way through the chips
while I recorded mental movies;
my camera-head started
to run out of film.
I'd had enough,
and I wanted to leave.

Then something happened
that had never happened before;
Steve got sick.
He was in the bathroom, the door shut, for a long time.
Anything that was in him was leaving him in a hurry.
I opened the door—
I shouldn't have.
Seeing him made *me* sick, and I was unable to help him.
I *couldn't* go near him,
and I didn't want to.
His pants were dropped to his ankles and
dipped into yellow, fetid puddles dotted with chunks of brown;
he was covered in vomit,
covered in feces.

I had no idea what was coming out of him,
but I knew
something was bad.
Very bad. So bad I knew I had made a mistake,
that I had come to this party.
That I had married him at nineteen.

His hair was matted in sweat.
His clothes stank, his breath reeked of puke.
I was able to get him on his feet
and, after a while, to the car.

We walked slowly in the heat.
He leaned on me

in the darkened street,
past barking dogs,
kids hanging out on stoops,
pizza shops,
classy restaurants.

We got to the car.
He sat beside me
in the passenger seat;
I was parked tightly between two cars.
I was ready to go,
when a taxi pulled up next to me,
discharged a passenger,
and my eye caught the specter
of a small person in the rearview mirror.
But then the image
disappeared.

I opened the door
and found a tiny, dark-haired woman
passed out
behind my car.
She barely had enough room to stand;
I helped her up.
She looked at me and
a small Irish voice whispered
from her four-foot-ten body,
"You aren't going to mug me, are you?"

At that moment
I realized that if I wanted to,
if I *really* wanted to,
I *could* mug her, *I could even kill her*.
I could leave her tiny, high-heeled, vulnerable body
behind my car,
make believe I didn't see her and—well—
just roll backward;

I could crush her,
squash her, the way
I accidentally killed a box turtle on a road in Idaho
during the summer of '73.
Feel the bump, then the shame.

And honestly, I *wanted* to kill her.
I wanted to kill Steve.
I wanted to kill drugs.
I wanted to kill anything
that could ever make me lose control
and be in the position
this woman was in,
at the mercy
of a stranger.
I realized I was powerful;
I was sober.

I took her by the arm,
escorted her to the entrance of her building,
and handed her over to the doorman.
"She's lucky, she's damn lucky
I saw her fall behind my car."
I returned.
I made sure there were no other dangers lurking,
no passed-out people,
no dog shit;
just piles of garbage
waiting to be picked up.

It was 1974.
It was Nixon.
It was Watergate.
It was a *raw* city,
before it got cleaned up,
before crime was down,
before the subways were reliable,

before drugs died out,
before window washer guys demanding money
were banned from the streets.
It was before recycling;
bulging black plastic bags created fortresses at curbs,
dented metal cans were overflowing
with paper,
rotting food,
and glass.

I could still hear Marvin in my head:
Don't you know
How sweet and wonderful life can be?

It was the year before
Steve died.

Fallen

Married in sixty-seven at nineteen,
a child whose life was built upon escape,
I thought that I attained a final dream,
but was awakened cruelly by my fate.
The man I wed was only twenty years,
so robust, strong, and blue-eyed that he be,
the honeymoon, so brief, had led to fears,
a premonition strong fell over me.
At dinner told the tale of quick demise,
his twenty-eight-year-old friend whose life was lost.
I found within my heart prescience disguised
and felt our fate was sealed at any cost.
And in eight years, true to life and breath,
mourned my husband, twenty-eight at his death.

Harlem on My Mind

**Shepard Hall
The City College of New York
Harlem, New York City, 1967
Photograph/Robert Kalish**

Skin

I had two mothers named *Pauline*,
one from Brooklyn, one from Harlem.
The one from Brooklyn was a little bit of a thing,
who raised two kids and worked full time.
The one from Harlem was a little bit of a thing,
who cleaned our apartment weekly.
Harlem-Pauline called Brooklyn-Pauline
Miss Pauline.
Some days when Pauline came
to push the mop and vacuum,
to stand tirelessly behind the ironing board,
I would pretend to be sick
and stay home from school.
I needed to watch her light her cigarette butts
with her head near the blue flame of the stove,
her eyelashes precariously close to the fire,
and previously singed.

For lunch she made herself deviled eggs.
I had never seen this before;
the creamy yellow in white nests, black pepper spots.
Pauline from Brooklyn never used black pepper.
I once hesitated to drink from a glass
I knew Pauline had put to her lips.
I didn't know she saw me.
She said,
"If I cut my skin, you would see white underneath.
If we both cut our skin, we bleed."

Pauline's tiny frame had a tobacco voice,
a boyfriend,
and a key to our apartment.
One day my sister came home from school

and found the door ajar,
and the little treasures of our lives
meticulously picked through,
butts left in the ashtray,
the pendant of lovebirds left to me
by Aunt Sarah,
gone. The small-faced diamond watch
my father had just given my mother
for their anniversary,
taken.
Hands had been in the Kotex box,
in the underwear.
My mother thought Pauline's boyfriend
entered and ran with our history
and security.

Years later, I was walking up the hill
on 145th Street, toward Convent Avenue,
to follow the white faces to the North Campus of C.C.N.Y.
The black sea parted,
and I saw Pauline.
Her tiny frame fed with deviled eggs,
her eyelashes singed,
she was walking down the hill in
the direction of
the A train, on her way
to stand behind an ironing board
and to push the mop and vacuum
for another family.

I kissed Pauline.
Her cheek was dry to my lips.

Take the A Train

My dad left me on the platform of the A train
on my first day of classes. My mother told him,
"Jack, take her." The truth was,
I had never traveled on the subway alone.

It was early in the morning
when the Chiclets smiled
little yellow, red, and green boxes
from the vending machines,
and the bums hunted for dimes
in the pay phones.

Then, like science fiction, the train
slowed at the platform and
the doors slid open and took me in.
Into a car that was strangely empty
for that hour of the morning.
I sat with the side of my forehead
leaning against stale glass.

At Forty-second Street,
the doors reeled in a large man
carrying a camel-colored coat over his heavy arm;
he caught me
and wedged me tighter into my corner;
then, there was pressure,
on my thigh.
Though under the cover of the coat,
his hand was visible in my mind
and translated into the language of
heat and teeth and claws
and gills and scales; a bottom feeder
at rest, with its red eyes open.

I knew it would be soon
when its weight
would shift
and would
bisect me.

At Fifty-ninth Street, a crowd entered,
the lights blinked, and in darkness,
we sped express to Harlem,
to 125th Street.

Now I was a small, bivalve urchin, stuck,
snapped shut,
tied down by seaweed and algae,
and drowning in an ocean of fear.

When I saw someone familiar,
my head drained of saltwater;
I wiped my eyes,
my shell opened, released me.
I grew legs,
and with a shove,
and a rush,
I was at the doors, devoured by a crowd
of other seventeen-year-olds,
who would trek uphill to the South Campus
and have English 101
for breakfast.

Hail Mary

Mary Jones was the Cleopatra of
Advanced French that summer.
Her skin was blackened by the Nile sun
in a previous life, when she was queen.
I once leaned against her arm over
Molière, while searching for my pen;
her skin was like
the fallen petals of a rose.

She was twenty-one, and a mother
with no husband,
this onyx jewel with
slow, smooth speech that
played the background jazz
as we spoke and walked along Convent Avenue.
She was going to leave the Mott Haven projects
in the South Bronx,
be a teacher,
was going to make it.

It was the year that
Who's Afraid of Virginia Woolf?
scandalized the screen,
and you had to be of age or
accompanied by an adult to see it.
I was seventeen.
Mary said, in her best torch song,
sibilant-enhanced melody:
"Don't worry, Susie. We'll just tell them
I'm your mother."

Theft

Someone stole the gold Cross pen
from atop my notebook
during speech class.
It was the beginning
of a period of suffering and transition.

Soon after,
it was announced that
the Reverend Martin Luther King
had been killed.
We filled the mazes of corridors
to hear a radio broadcast
in Shepard Hall,
the crown of the C.C.N.Y. North Campus,
the building that looks like
a huge, regal fortress of
dark-brick chocolate cake, adorned
with drips of hard white icing.

The City College of New York:
a place that has been feeding
thousands of immigrants
and their children
the sweetness of knowledge
and the promise of a future.
A place where all classes and creeds
and their progeny commuted
hopefully,
daily,
through catacomb-tunnels of subways
from all the hungry places of the city.

We lined the floors with our bodies, books, and jackets,
our legs curled under us and
our shoulders, defeated.
We were ants in tunnels with no work to do,
no leader to follow, no queen,
no King.

When the public address system went silent
and left us with static in our heads,
we dispersed from the winding hallways
lined with door after door of mahogany and frosted glass;
you didn't have to press your face
and squint against translucent light
to see that
all chairs were vacant.

It was right after someone took my gold Cross pen.
The one I got for my birthday.

Flaws

I sat on the A train,
the last seat next to the door
and the conductor's booth,
guarding the prize of my life
on the run up to Harlem.

My left hand was clenched shut;
my ring finger was bent to the palm,
sweating with its neighbors,
tight, beneath the thumb.

The train sped express between Fifty-ninth
and 125th Street, screeching along curved metal,
its toothy windows rattling,
lights blinking as we passed over dead track.

In the flashes of dark I opened my hand—
as if holding a butterfly that might escape—
to check that *it* was still there,
and to protect it from those who might try to
make off with it.

In the small expanse of offered light,
for the nanoseconds it was fed,
facets bounced and played, made sparks,
like the metal wheels against metal rails.
When the cold bulbs reignited the voyage
I gently splayed my fingers,
like a blooming peony
or water lily,
and the pistil became a diamond
turned inward on my ring finger,
wet;

its mirror image
of prongs and pear shape
pressed into my
palm.

I was on my way to the South Campus;
it was a long hike up the Convent Avenue hill
that made me pant against history
and French literature books,
breathless with fatigue and fear.
Well before the Harlem Renaissance,
my route was lined with tenements, derelicts,
broken bottles,
men hanging out on stoops.
Weeds against fences of vacant lots.

Finally, when the gates opened to castles, moats, and grass,
I was delirious with giddiness, joy, youth.
On my way to class, in the middle of the city—
in the depths of a poverty area
in 1966,
wearing
the uninsured
pear-shaped diamond engagement ring
that I had just gotten the day before.
I was eighteen years old.
I would be married at nineteen.

It was not long after,
upon close examination of the stone,
initially pear, now tear,
that one could see
several grains of carbon within,
and a chip along the side.

Dyre Avenue Days

Windows black with soot.
Try to look through the paths
etched by rain at a sky forever attempting
to be blue,
never passing gray,
as you withstand the
hundred-twenty-decibel level scream
of the elevated train,
the Number 5,
the Dyre Avenue line.

You are the voyeur
of the balloon-letters,
the spray-painted buildings,
of the subliminal flashes of factory workers
all named by the Caribbean,
tied together with threads colored
Carmen, Marisol, Maria, Chica,
as the train races, singing and swaying,
South Bronx South Bronx South Bronx,
and does the *pasodoble* on the curved track
around the twists and turns of the blackened tenements
bodega bodega bodega bodega.

One day, a mechanical mistake;
you almost got sucked out when the doors
flew open and the air was cool and
green with spring, and gaping windows looked at you.
You were racing, careening, past windows holding
the faces of papacitos, waiting alone with the TV
for mamas to come home
and put up the arróz con pollo.
Mammas,
their eyes strained,

their backs round,
and their fingers aching
from feeding the hungry machines.

Your heart pounds as you grab for the pole,
and you cover your mouth,
as you realize that
the train almost took you,
almost pulled you out
into the clarity of the moment.
Maybe you missed the omen,
perhaps it flashed by too quickly?
Did you see
the South Bronx King?
Soft, black, and brown,
at regal, rigid attention,
someone's friend and guardian,
a German shepherd,
straight and long,
hanging by the leash around its neck,
past the
kicking,
muscle-strangling struggle;
the dog,
dangling,
high above the
bodega bodega bodega bodega bodega
from the fire escape.
Its subjects go about their business below,
but you were privy
to the future of
the South Bronx.

Part 3
Beyond the Pale

For Orvieto, Italy

Cathedral
Orvieto, Italy, 1983
Photograph/Susan Margulies Kalish

As the traveler who has once been from home is wiser than
he who has never left his own doorstep, so a knowledge
of one other culture should sharpen our ability to scrutinize
more steadily, to appreciate more lovingly, our own.
~Margaret Mead

Birthing at Bocuse

Illustration/Susan Margulies Kalish

Birthing at Bocuse

1

Outside Lyons, France
July 27, 1982

Chez Paul Bocuse, a five-star event
just outside of Lyons,
serves one hundred-fifty-dollar dinners
of endless courses:
soups that wear a pastry chef's hat,
swimming pools of butter with drowning snails,
goose paté from ripened, grain-fed, white honkers,
wine and more wine,
and the intercourses:
little scoops of sorbet.
Cheeses and breads,
carts of custardy pastries,
and superior chocolates
from Maurice Bernachon,
The chocolatier of Lyons.
This is the place,
the place where I seared my mouth on the soup
and feared I was going to use the wrong fork.
The place where I assented
when le garçon recommended
la specialité de la maison:
chicken cooked in a
pig's bladder.

2

Reconsideration

But now I have second thoughts,
and my head reels from
the fog of cigar smoke,
the murmuring around me
of the incomprehensible and *proper* French,
the wine,
and more wine.
My nasal interior rebels and swells,
leaving my lungs spasming for air.
I am having a panic attack ...

Into my consciousness creeps a vision of
comfort and safety:
America. Its golden arches:
McDonald's.
I have been transformed into
a soldier who is about to meet the enemy:
my dinner.
Then fight to the death,
en garde!,
at this very table;
I wonder:
Is a chicken cooked in a pig's bladder
armed with a bayonet?

3

Religion

Oh God, please help me,
Next time I promise to stay home,
stick close to the kosher deli,
order hot pastrami on rye with those fat fries
the size of
Paul Bunyan's fingers.
Just don't let me faint and fall
at the sight of a pig's bladder,
face-first into my foie gras.
Amen.

4

Labor

I start to take
deep Lamaze, rapid-panting breaths
as a silver dome-covered tray is escorted to my table
by an entourage of waiters.
The dome reflects a terror-stricken woman who
is about to lose the first six courses of her meal,
on the floral carpet.
Waiter Number One raises the highly polished dome
in slow motion;
my life revisits me in a rapid succession
of flashing film clips.
There it is: a five-star, smooth, pink mound on a tray,
a pregnant woman's stomach, without the woman.
This is the one hundred and fifty dollar
chicken cooked in a pig's bladder,
(it sounded a lot better in French),
but I don't see a chicken.
And now my eyes are totally dilated:
breathe, breathe!
Waiter Number Two whisks the cover away.
Waiter Number Three presents the huge tray,
while Waiter Number Four approaches the
pregnant stomach,
the smooth, pink hump
(surrounded by little diced white and orange vegetables)
with a knife!
I think: This hump must be in its ninth month of gestation.
And then I realize, ready or not:
I am about to witness a birth.

Or maybe a murder.

5

Birth and Revelation

Waiter Number Four lifts a paper-thin corner
of pink bladder membrane
with a knife
and nicks it,
an act of a covenant,
a circumcision?
It shrivels,
like the Wicked Witch of the West,
and reveals:
a chicken.
A regular, normal, Frank Purdue
oven-stuffer roaster from which
more of the diced vegetables are spilling.
The chicken, a cornucopia of joy.
The chicken, a familiar vision, at thirty-nine cents a pound.
Le poulet.
The waiter, having completed the C-section,
now carves like an experienced surgeon.

6

Renaissance (My Rebirth)

My breathing is now regular;
my nasal passages are retreating,
permitting oxygen
into my lungs, aorta, extremities.
My body relaxes;
the six previous courses are no longer a threat
to the carpet.
I look to heaven with thanks.
Birthing can sure make one hungry.

Paris, 2001
Illustration/Susan Margulies Kalish

Who Have Become Crows

The Senegalese men,
tall, thin,
lining the streets,
selling trinkets,
postcards,
wind-up birds with red, fragile wings.

They flock to the base of
the Eiffel Tower
to hawk their wares to tourists,
their skin so dark,
their teeth so bright,
their eyes so determined,
yet desperate,
seeking a sale:
cartes postales, dix francs.

From afar come the sirens, the flashing lights,
the blue uniforms, the round, flat-topped caps:
The police!
Running,
weaving
through the crowds
and under the huge, iron claws.
Pursuing,
fleeing,
flapping.

A white, plastic bag
crackles,
inflates,
and is released to the wind,
briefly taking flight,
then spilling

gold and silver key rings,
abandoned
by the Senegalese men
who have become
crows.

In the microcosm
of a butter-broiled truffle,
half the size of a human face,
a tiny maggot,
small, white, blind worm,
its head, red and eyeless,
is stopped dead in its tracks.

MOON MAGGOT

Siena, Italy, 1983
Photography/Illustration
Susan Margulies Kalish

Moon Maggot

1

In the microcosm
of a butter-broiled truffle,
half the size of a human face,
a tiny maggot, small, white, blind,
is stopped dead in its tracks.
Its head is red and eyeless.
It was searching blindly in
my prima piatta.

The tiny wanderer is scraped away.
I eat as
the Sienese air cools
and darkens
around the piazza, now the eye of the universe,
and the moon observes
the deep brown umber.
Ancient walls echo with voices.
The swallows scream
and circle about the rooftops,
now pink, now gold, now pale violet.

The Palio was here;
charging horses and riders
now replaced
by the slow evening promenade
of arm-linked couples, running children,
and flirting, laughing groups of
mouth-covering adolescents.
Year, after year, after year,
the cool façades
watch silently;
the view never changes.

2

Earlier in the afternoon,
wandering the streets and alleys,
I photographed seven smiling children
who were rolling a small potato
into chalk boxes drawn on
the stone-paved street.
A mother watched them from
behind the red geraniums
in her window,
her arms crossed beneath her breasts.

3

At times, I feel the subtle isolation
of a stranger with a camera.
At mealtimes, when I
pass the open windows
and plates and forks and glasses
sing from within,
I smell the warmth, the connections,
the continuity, the operatic relationships.
I feel the hunger;
I try to visually steal those inside.
But I am the moon maggot,
stopped dead,
broiling in the sun.

Part 4
Footprints

Grandmother, Sophie Kolsadt Wasserman, ca. 1900
Margulies Family archive

Needles

1

Sophie Kolsadt—
born in Kiev,
in the province of Kishenev,
in the 1890s
when one day it was part of Russia,
another day, Romania—
was never allowed to go to school
because she was a girl.
But she could sew,
and when she was six,
a tiny girl with long blonde braids and green eyes,
she sewed for
the Tsar of Russia.
At Christmas, she was given a dress.

2

I saw a museum exhibit
of the Russian royal family's treasures.
There were gold Fabergé eggs that opened and
housed intricate music boxes and dancing ballerinas,
encrusted with jewels and inlaid enamels.
There were garments of silk, awash in seas of tiny seed pearls,
heavy woven brocades of gold and silver threads
trimmed with feathers and furs.

I wondered which of the Romanovs wore
these garments,
these diamond tiaras en tremblant;
was it Anastasia?
As I looked at these,
I caught my green-eyed
reflection in the glass
of case after case, and I wondered
how many of the billions of
tiny silken stitches
my grandma Sophie may have sewn.

The Horrible End of Roseann Quinn

I can still see your post-hippie-days,
funny face,
hear your laugh,
recall your curly, wild, Irish-red hair
and your funky clothes,
the knit hat and scarf
of browns and yellows,
the granny glasses,
the funny, fuzzy, fake fur coat.
And how we sat together
in graduate classes at Hunter College
in the evenings of 1970.

You had a limp,
I later learned, from
childhood polio, and
humor that released you
from your childhood
of religious bondage.

You lifted me with stories,
like the one of the deaf child in your class
at St. Joseph's in the Bronx;
you told him there would be a party
at school,
and the little boy dutifully
brought his contribution:
a bottle of his dad's
best booze.
Or maybe it was cerveza.

You were thin and young,
lanky, boney, bent,
mini-skirted,

Upper West-Sided,
in your twenties, and
about to die.

Judith Rossner wrote a book
about you:
Looking for Mr. Goodbar.

And then there was the movie.
The theatres were packed,
the audiences watched,
never realizing
you were real.
That as
Diane Keaton (you)
and Richard Gere (him)
fucked in your single-girl bed,
and she (you) yelled, "Sweet Jesus!"
when she (you) climaxed,
escaping from her (your) strict Catholic dogma,
that you,
funny little Rosie,
were real.

That on New Year's Day 1973,
he, John Wayne Wilson,
tore your
Roseann Quinn soul
with sharp objects
and crushed your skull and face,
sweet Rosie,
with the heavy bust someone had sculpted of you
that you kept near your bed.
That you were real, and funny, and adorable, but
the police could not tell if you had a face
or how long you existed.
And we voyeurs left the movie,

our hands damp with tears
and blood,
because we knew you,
or knew others like you,
who met grifters in bars,
then took them home.

And that you were real.

Love Song for Liviu Librescu

Liviu, I Liviu, I love you.
How many times have I told you that over so many years, my dear,
my sweet man? When I learned English, I would say
I Liviu!
It was our secret,
our love secret. It made you laugh like a child.
It was so long ago. "Roumania, Roumania."
We loved to sing that song.
We were betrayed by our country:
Roumania! How they gave us to the Nazis.
How you worked 'til your hands bled,
and you almost starved in the labor camp.
Transnistra.
The living hell.
The fear.
The hunger.
The bodies toppling into pits.
But you survived, you endured, you defied.
Ah, smart Liviu, so smart always.
We fell in love at the Foscani ghetto.
Can you remember the first time you saw me?
I turned. I was so shy.
You knew the meaning of life, of survival.
You put the camp behind you.
You put me in front of you.
Three hundred, eighty thousand Jews perished in Roumania;
we did not!
You soared in spirit and work and mind.
How brilliant an engineer! How brave a man!
You refused to swear your soul to the regime, and in turn,
we were not allowed to leave for Israel.
Hadn't we suffered enough? Would we ever be free?
But Menachim Begin helped us.
We moved in 1978.

Aeronautics.
You were so well known in your field,
known all over the world.
So many nights I brought you glasses of tea
while you were thinking, writing,
paper after paper.
Hundreds of acclaimed works.
Then that special year:
1985, the sabbatical year we went to
the United States, and our Joe attended technical school,
Virginia Tech!
We stayed in Virginia.
You became a professor at the school Joe attended.
How proud I was!
We had a good life, my Liviu, I Liviu.
We survived so much pain.
So much terror.

We were finally at peace.
And now I must go on without you.
I do not know how.

I know what happened when you heard the shots.
You thought of the dogs.
You thought of the guards, the clubs,
the whistles, the blood.
You were wearing your gray stripes.
You smelled it, death, with every ring of the bullets.
Your campmates became faces in an Edvard Munch painting.
"Quickly!" you said, "Barricade the door! Push! All you can!"

As the fog of death poured under the threshold like water, seeping
and hissing like a snake, you told them: "Jump!"
And they did, from the window.
The sound of their cracking, splitting bones,
tearing skin on glass,
deafened you to the gunshot you couldn't run from.

I Liviu, my love, my hero.
Librescu.
Free.

Professor Liviu Librescu was seventy-six years old, and a Holocaust survivor. He died by gunshot, trying to save his students during the Virginia Tech massacre, April 16, 2007.

Bog Man

Illustration/Susan Margulies Kalish

The Bog Man

1

Ca. 470 BC

The Bog man:
his skin dried, weathered, withered,
leathered.
Peat man,
brown, dusty man.
Ancient, Celtic man. Boy?
Your face confused, contorted,
eye sockets sunken,
eyes almost gone,
blind man.
You walked over green fields,
you tended white sheep,
you planted brown seeds.
You, man or boy, danced,
one with time,
one with peat,
one with
leathered skin,
cloak, cap,
holding your walking stick,
you came out of your hut.

2

1974

Young man, tall man,
golden hair, blue eyes.
Once ran, once flew,
once danced.
Young man, tall man, young man.
Thin man, old man.
Walks along the street
in big shoes too heavy
to lift; scrape, scrape, slowly.
The brown leather coat,
a balloon billow cloak.
The air is blue cold
but warming to spring.
The brown leather cap
close to your eyes,
shading them from gold sun.
Tread slowly, young man,
old man.
Slower still.
Hold your walking stick, my shoulder,
and tend the lambs on the street.
Lift the clown shoes, raise your feet.
We're almost home.

3

Your feet too old,
your heart too young
to pump the blood of many
unknown soldiers.
Your innards, knotted, deny you food,
your exterior belies your youth;
lips cracked and leathered,
long fingers, white on white,
your ears and eyes
play tricks,
your gray matter misfires.
You're the prisoner of wires,
you descend,
down, down
deeper into
the peat sheet.
Hungry again?
Then bite the Loch Ness monster!
Send forth green,
spew it, spit it.
Spring green, hunter's green.
Bile.

4

Return to the forest where
it is dense and safe.
Can't? What?
A tired prisoner?
Tethered, tube-tied captive?
The forest elves hold you down
and strip you, pluck each hair,
Return you to youth,
shaven,
your face, your body,
alien.
Your penis rough, small, red, rubber,
a dead animal lying on its side.
You decide.
You need nothing.
Not your eyes, or your ears.
Only your hand,
which you empower
to pull out
the tube.

5

The bog man.
His skin dried, weathcred, withered,
leathered.
Peat man,
brown, dusty man.
Ancient Celtic man. Boy?
Did you huddle by a fire?
Did you hunger for stone soup?
Did you walk through heather
on that day, your feet
wrapped in rags
to ward off
the cold.
Was the ground
spongy with rain?
Who did this to you?
Your teeth are brown
and broken,
your ear detached.
The forest elves?
Hold the walking stick
tightly.
Don't despair.
I look at you.
You avert your eyes.
I avert mine.
Don't catch me!
I am embarrassed by my own
curious gaze.
But tell me:
Who tied

the rope
around
your neck
and
threw you
into
the
bog?

6

Let me open your glass house
and remove that frayed rope.
There, that's better;
now you can rest.
Close your eyes,
the tubes are gone,
turn on your side,
pull your knees to your chest.
Hold the walking stick,
old man, young man,
Dublin museum man,
bog man brown,
go back
to the lambs.

Article in the *New York Times*
August 8, 1936

Freddy Osborn, Kansas City, 1936

You don't need to worry about me, sister,
I am nine years old,
and I am going to
buy a horse and a wagon
and go way off and live by myself.

My sister Helen is eleven, and she's been takin' care of us
since last week; she stands tall and proud.
Some ladies and men are here lookin' us over;
Betty is six, George is four, and Norma Jean is three.
Nobody wants me. But I don't care.
Helen told them she read a book about those orphanages,
she said she wouldn't let us go.
That we all got to stay together.
We are all good children,
she said so.
We can play the combs and make music,
sounds pretty good.

They all want little Norma Jean.
George needs a spankin' but not me.
Just tell me nice what I got to do, I'll be good.

But I can always buy a horse and a wagon
and go way off and live by myself.
This all wouldn't a been happenin'
if step-daddy didn't a killed mama
with that gun.
Shot her in the face and
then himself. We all seen it.
I miss my mama.
I can always go and buy a horse and a wagon
and go way off
and live by myself.

For Suzanne Loew
1949–1989

Photograph/Susan Margulies Kalish, ca. 1978

Let us be grateful to people who make us happy,
they are the charming gardeners who make our souls bloom.
~Marcel Proust

Makeover

For Suzanne Loew

I have seen you in dreams.
You are young and beautiful,
sitting in a car, giggling with your date
in front of your building
off Fifth Avenue,
waiting for alternate side parking to end,
having martinis that you brought down on a tray.

I still grab at the moment, the one in my mind,
where I can see you laughing,
tossing the perfectly cut curls,
white teeth surrounded by red lips—
a color by Estée Lauder.
You are wearing your two-tone
Baume and Mercier watch,
the one you debated about, not sure if you deserved,
bought with inheritance money
your father left.
Your father, who left.

You would have been
sixty
on January seventeenth;
instead you are keeping
your father company in a graveyard
in Hampton, Connecticut, on a hill
near the farm.
And so, since you were forty,
I haven't seen you,
but I hear you talking to me all the time.
I know you are standing behind me,
pushing me when I hesitate,

guiding me around curves.

Your friend Claudia
has taught me to see you in miracles.
After you left us,
a rainbow appeared outside her door.
The electricity in her house rebelled for days
when she entered the room,
flashing for no reason; messages,
we hoped.
And then the rainbows followed me
as birthday gifts,
as signs of strength when
I was in need,
as a reminder to be joyous,
as you were
when you sang
"You Are My Sunshine."

It was July 1989
when you came to visit;
I see us standing, talking
in front of the post office
on Main Street, Flushing,
where you became the keeper of my secrets.
Now you know all secrets.

We walked to Stern's
for Shiseido makeovers,
and the woman behind the counter said,
"I bet with your coloring, you wear
a lot of navy blue."
She covered your ruddy, healthy face
with the paleness of the moon,
removing all traces of sun,
and your black hair shone like a
background for stars.

Your face faded into porcelain and
I looked at you
and knew—
you were going to die.

Weeks later.

Why would you,
a marathon runner in your prime,
a single, New York lady
who grew up with milk cows,
why would you get on that plane?
Why would you work so hard all summer
and then choose to go so far?
How could you
sit for so many hours aloft,
with your marathon runner friend,
and alight in Sydney for a vacation,
while I watched *Arsenio Hall*
and changed diapers
on Cape Cod?
How could you get off a plane,
go to a hotel,
leave your bags, and
go out for a walk
at 7:30 AM?

How could you
stand at a corner, on an empty street,
waiting to cross?
How could a car
plow into a parked car?
And,
how could a parked car
pick you up
and take you home?

I need to know if you are fine.

I have no more words,
I am out of phrases, I am bereft of sentences.
My heart can only muster questions.

I went to your apartment
to help pick out your clothes
for the event that would bring
two hundred people together.
You were their best friend.
Sarah was already there.
She opened the door, and the smell of flowers
invited me in.
But there were none to be seen.

We searched like robbers to remove valuables
and couldn't decide if you should wear
the white suit with the floral blouse
or the running suit with your Avias.
I thought you should be comfortable,
for you still had a lot of running to do.

When I went into the bathroom,
it was as though you had just come in,
about to step into the shower,
breathing,
sweating,
glowing from a run,
your bra hanging
behind the bathroom door,
on the knob.
Sitting quietly on the sink
was the Shiseido face cream we bought
just a few weeks before.
I opened it.
It had been touched once.

I could see your fingerprint
clearly; it was suspended on the pink gel
as though one finger was gingerly
testing the waters.
Not yet ready to jump in.

Several black hairs were lying akimbo in the sink;
others were twisted and coiled,
trapped in your brush.

You left in such a hurry.

I saw myself in your mirror.

I knew that somewhere,
someone was saying,
"You look great in navy."

Part 5
From the Observatory

For Robert Kalish and Evan Kalish

Photograph/Jack Margulies, ca. 1949

I am turned into a sort of machine for observing facts and grinding out conclusions.
~Charles Darwin

Evolution

Bang!

Birth. Fire. Water. Earth.
Cretaceous, spacious, bodacious, dearth—
buds, plants, pollen; cries
for bees, moths, butterflies.
Homosapiens: planters, farmers, sowers;
buzzers flying, busy growers;
petals, stamens, pistils, honey;
hives, harvest, workers, money.
Cell phones ringing? GPS?
Fly too high like Icarus?
Hives are empty, won't be long:
barren fields, dry and wan,
sunspots? warming? global spawn?
Look again, the bees are gone.
On Einstein's Earth, years left there's four—
once the bees are nevermore.

Bang.

Lunacy

1

The butter moon
waits to be spread
across the sky,
now black bread.
For brief moments,
the view will last,
my eyes fill with
this bright repast.
And then with hunger
my heart does long
and bite
by bite
the moon
is
gone.

2

Hughes, Plath:
wrath.
Rivera, Kahlo:
halo.
Rodin, Claudell:
hell.
Man on the moon:
I am so cold.

Yellow Jell-O

See the picture of
the family in the ad
in *Ladies' Home Journal*?
There they are!
Clustered at supper time around the table
with their moon faces.
Father has a white shirtsleeve
rolled up above his Hamilton watch,
his tie is still on.
Mother, perfect and coiffed, in her apron
with the little chef's hats on it,
serves meat loaf
moistened with ketchup,
and mashed potatoes,
buttered green peas nestled nearby.
How warm a scene.
And then it is more perfect!
Mother brings out the lemon dessert;
it wriggles free of its mold like
a butterfly emerging wet from its cocoon
and shimmies dangerously and provocatively.
The 2.5 children can see themselves in it,
their smiles reflected, distorted.
The family is contained by it,
protected by it.
Look through it;
it's like those yellow sunglasses that make
cloudy days hurt your eyes and
make you squint in pain.
That's the scene on the shiny page
that smells like fresh ink,
where the world is safe
and people live
in yellow Jell-O.

Atlas

Follow the highways,
interstates,
expressways
of the lines on my face,
the arteries of my body.
Stop at the green lights of my eyes
and go at the sight of red blood.
I know
my hair is a tangle of weeds, brambles,
and memories of fingers.
My heart is a rotary to which veins go.
Some of my countries have been earthquaked
or glaciered,
shifting south
when once north,
creating civil unrest.

Craters have formed where
I have cried,
filling lakes
now barren,
the desert cracked where
I have laughed.
Uplifted like mountains
by turbulence below,
I am filled by a lava flow.

Fall

Leaves,
to flip through,
fill up,
scribble, dabble, crumple, toss.
Hold:
ideas, chewed gum, lone words, erasures,
pencil shavings, love notes, footprints,
frustration, triumph.
Three-hole punched,
right-margined,
plastic-wrapped.
Ripped open.

Divide and conquer.
Into big rings
held fast.
They wait.

Married Life

For Ogden Nash

Married life is never boring
when my husband dear is snoring.
A yowl, a squeal, a cry, a bark,
all come at me from the dark;
I dream I'm in Jurassic Park.

Married life is never trite
when I go to sleep at night,
here they come—the growls, the blows,
I push and kick him with my toes;
in desperation clamp his nose.

Married life is so inviting
when my sleep his snarks are spiting.
Awake, his love is so adoring,
but in bed his throat is roaring;
I rarely know what is in storing.

Married life is never lonely
when you have your one and only.
Grit your teeth and get the plugs,
write a poem and pace the rugs;
glass of milk? Resort to drugs?

Married life is so courageous
perhaps his snores became contagious.
Although I do not make a peep,
I'm told he dreams of cars that beep;
I *never* make noise in *my* sleep.

Cats Took Over My House

Cats took over my house!
Cats took over my house!

I never sleep;
they tickle my feet.

The couch I mourn;
the leather is torn.

They run and they zoom
by the light of the moon.

There's never a day
they don't want to play.

There's nary a mouse,
just my fur-covered spouse.

Cats took over my house!

There's 9-Lives, always,
and Friskies' Buffets.

They rub on my leg;
for turkey they beg.

I cry and I blink
when their box starts to stink.

They knock over clocks
while tossing my socks.

Cats took over my house!

They're eating the plants
and go into a trance.

Newspaper they shred
on the floor—*that* I dread.

They twitch and they scheme;
must be having a dream.

They tear and they rip—
it has been quite a trip.

I say, *nevermore!*
but you know I adore
those

cats that took over my house!

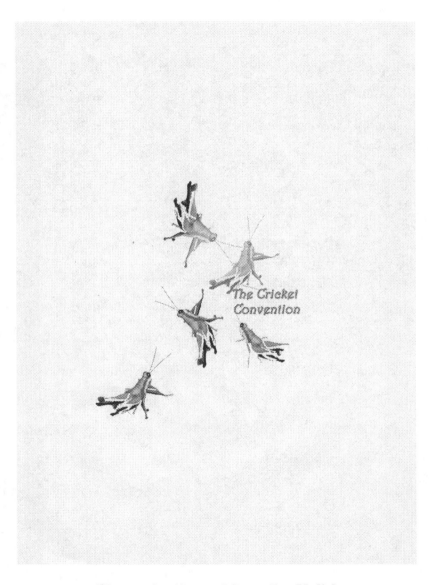

The Cricket Convention

Illustration/Susan Margulies Kalish

The Cricket Convention

1

How comforting
to hear the din
of the crickets' convention
at 4:00 AM.
The joy, chatter,
purring, singing, rowdy
white noise
at the gray hour between
night and day.
Lie awake and marvel
at their fearless innocence.
I think:
How lucky they are.

2

November first and it is 5:00 AM;
I awaken and hear the call
of one lonely cricket
who hadn't the sense to hide
from the world
at the designated time.
Holden Caulfield would ask:
"What happens to the crickets in winter?"
I think:
What will happen to mankind?
And:
Why isn't man kind?
Then wonder:
If I could fit where the crickets go,
would I emerge next spring
to sing
at the crickets' convention?

3

When I squint my ears into the seeming silence,
to find my heart's quiet,
to see the warmth of summer evenings
slowly leaving,
I hear Christmas coming.
It is the crickets.
Hiding in the tall grass,
sharing daily talk,
standing at their street corners
ringing little sleigh bells.

Before the First Frost

The rosebush produced one final beauty,
fighting against time.
I cut it brazenly,
with a pair of scissors from the desk.
Tiny thorns
tried to fight back, and
its thin stem
maintained a defiant posture.

What makes a rose still want grow in November?
Do roses fear dying?
It was standing tall, proud, alone,
still spunky from summer,
maybe a teenager,
peachy, against crisp brown,
smelling of citrus and attar.
It missed curfew;
it mocked the season.

It's supposed to get quite cold on Wednesday,
the first frost;
I scurried around
bringing in what I could.
Blooming geraniums, still flowering,
leaves caught in their hair.
A potted pepper plant with a last hanger-on,
green, compact, and shiny.
Holding fast.

Where could I put them all?

I picked the last of the cherry tomatoes.
I don't have the heart
to pluck out the green stems

of soon-to-die plants.
I just
don't
have
the heart.

And now the roses
will go to sleep.

What the Birds Know

Through the back window, the apple tree
stands, rooted and bare,
beseeching the sky for the sun it recalls,
reaching with black arms,
dripping with cold rain.

It wears the bird feeder; I hooked it
into an old vacant wound,
like one Bohemian earring,
and to it go fat, crested blue jays,
bright cardinals—the females in drab.
Small brown sparrows and red robins
take the feed from soil below;
the squirrels, wide-jerking-tailed
and gray-fluffed, yank and pull and spill the seeds,
changing the birds' dance,
manipulating the food chain and creating a hierarchy.
Seeds and wings scatter.

The grass is still green but soon will be frosted,
covered by hoary leaf remnants.
Entombed in clarity,
encased by remembrance of digging moles
now asleep and waiting, it will crack and crunch
underfoot.
For months.

It is just the start, merely the beginning,
before the intent of white blankets,
brown melt,
black glaze,
blue reflection,
pale sun.
Just the initiation.
The birds know.

Couples

Dedicated to my friends

Photography/Illustration
Susan Margulies Kalish

No person is your friend who demands your silence, or denies
your right to grow.
~Alice Walker

One Evening in July 2006

Tanglewood

He had that Hollywood look,
the tan and lined outdoor face that said, "Maybe I'm an actor."
In fact, he reminded me of Patrick Swayze in *Dirty Dancing*.
He wore a tight T-shirt,
slightly faded like army drabs;
on closer inspection I could see
that there was a pattern of swirls of blue and green and mottled brown,
like marble.
He bent his dark and silver head of tousled hair toward the woman
with the medium-length blond, wavy hair.

She was youthful, slim, toned.
His wife. Or his lover.
Maybe in her fifties.
She could have been his *Frances Baby Houseman*
years after they met in the Catskills
and he transformed her innocence
by teaching her the dance moves,
lifting her over his head so she could soar
arms extended
after she ran
and leaped into his waiting arms.

Now
that image sat tamed,
five rows ahead of me at Tanglewood
(a far cry from the old Catskill hotels
where children of Jewish, Irish, Italian, and German immigrants
escaped the oppressive city heat)
the night that Seiji Ozawa conducted Mahler's *Second*.
She couldn't see, so she moved several seats over and
claimed an empty seat at the end the row—

to better inhale the baton, the breeze,
the notes.

Their separation was like a
smiling mouth with missing teeth.
Almost shocking after having been so close,
they were apart with empty seats between them, yet
they were still connected by music.
After the passion of each movement ebbed and flowed
and washed over them, the performance ended.
She moved back to his side,
stood and clapped
and clapped, with her tanned hands
and toned arms, and clapped
then sat next to him through the third round of bows.

I could see their heads move together,
they exchanged a word
as the stage light illuminated their hair
like halos,
then pulled apart to make room
for her left hand,
the back of which
gently ran
up and down
his cheek.

Lori and Dean
at the funeral of Lori's Mother
2006

Shadows

Lori's been through two marriages;
the first seemed normal enough,
to Larry, a college professor.
But it ended. Childless.

And then there was the second, to a rock musician,
who also had been through a previous marriage;
they produced a son and
raised him on the milk of
the Sex Pistols and on various forms of
secondhand smoke,
causing him to suffer from attention deficit disorder;
he went on meds so he could function in school.

No one could figure out why the first marriage ended
and why the second one lasted as long as it did,
considering the drugs, and that he didn't work;
and she, *she* was a professional, who
supported them and bought them a home.
This second marriage ended
in Madison, Wisconsin, where state law gave him half of
everything.
The wife and son were unforgiving.

Then, in her fifties, she found Dean.
She was still long and lanky, and youthful,
but with graying bangs.
When I saw Lori at her mother's funeral,
her hair had been dyed a washed-out brown.
She was now sixty, and on this day, distraught.

Dean stood by her side at the service.
He enveloped her in his arms,
making her look small and vulnerable.
She was.

He rested his arm on the back of the bench
and created a niche for her to take refuge in.
She was like a bird that had fallen
from a nest
with no mother to comfort her.
She yielded to his protection,
his strength, his wholeness.
He pulled her close,
never thinking that
she was Jewish and he was Christian,
that she was born in New York and he was from Minnesota,
that she was a Democrat and he a Republican.
It mattered not that she was thin and he was beefy.
They were a comfort to one another
in the battlefield of opposites.
They balanced, leaned on, supported, nurtured, and fed off
all that they could find positive within their differences.

After the funeral
and a mourning meal in her mother's backyard,
they stood together, entwined in front of the house
her parents bought in 1951,
a house that will likely be bought by developers, demolished,
and replaced.
This was the house she grew up in,
that she left for failed marriages,
that she came back to, now, as an orphan.

The moon was rising;
when the pale light touched their faces,
it blurred the past and the present,
and cast the solidity of their forms as one large shadow

and revealed
what wasn't clear in the brightness of the sun.
Dean was only in his thirties,
and that the long shadow they created
mirrored the length
of their future.

Asian couple at the Shake Shack,
Madison Square Park, New York City
on a Sunday in August 2006

Labels

The line for the burgers, fries, shakes, and cones
was like a snake,
winding and twisting around
people,
trash cans, and
little running children.

It was thick and thin,
as people stood in twos, or threes or fours,
grinding their feet in the dusty path
in anticipation of *the Best Burgers in New York*.
It was a Sunday,
and businessmen were home watching *the game*;
running shoes were de rigueur.
People studied the menu,
handwritten and weathered on an easel.
They walked up to it
as if they were meeting royalty,
bowing to it
as their dogs yanked at their leashes
or, if they had no dog, there was a baby tossing toys from a stroller.
Usually the babies and the dogs became acquainted.

On the line, Asian manikins: a man and a woman,
perfection on a Sunday.
She, more formal
than necessary,
he, formally informal.
They ordered, waited; when their number was called,
they picked up the burgers, fries, and shakes that were

wedged into cardboard carriers
and carefully walked over the dusty pebbles and
sat at one of the small metal tables.

He stood tall;
his head was shaved, and thick Cartiers framed his eyes.
His arms were strong from exercising;
red and green tattoos ran up and down them.
Chains hung from his neck and another from the belt loop of
tight jeans ending in
a clanging of keys.
His name, according to his T-shirt,
was Comme des Garçons 2001.

Her black hair was pulled up and off her face revealing
15 mm Mikimoto pearl earrings;
she guarded her pale green and turquoise patterned silk
shirtwaist (with lace petticoat artfully revealed at the hem)
from the ketchup; she tapped her gold jeweled
Manolo flats against the table leg.
He had his chocolate shake, she, her Fiji water.
He examined his thick burger; she studied her fries before dipping
them in the small white paper cup filled with ketchup.
And when they were done,
they patted their mouths with white paper napkins
and cleaned off the table.
She picked up her Kate Spade bag, and they walked off on
the rocky path.
They were perfection.
They never said a word.

Colleen and Ron, Manhattan Theatre Club, Seats C102 and 104
Sunday, September 24, 2006

Chains

Though we had never met before, we were comfortable
with theater talk:
playwrights, directors, actors, subscriptions.
They were a handsome couple in their fifties or sixties,
unselfconscious about their appearance,
yet well put-together,
even-tempered,
humorous, endearing.

They sat to my left.
The first thing I noticed about Colleen
was her lilting voice and red hair. She said
she did commercials and some acting.
Ron jiggled his legs as he spoke;
he, too, articulate, with a good, strong voice.

We sat in the dark and laughed together,
the play was well written and well acted
but at times complex and confusing, so we
compared notes during intermission.
We had each caught different subtleties
that we pooled.

Then talk about animals;
Colleen said she had
dogs for over forty years.
At her feet, a chain rattled and up came the black head of a young
Labrador Retriever, a Seeing-Eye dog.
She insisted on parking her warm face in Colleen's lap;
Ron pushed the dog back down to the floor.
"She's bored," he said, "but she has to learn."

Ötzi, the Iceman, and Erika Simon, the German hiker,
at their reunion in the Otzal Alps,
September 19, 1991

Love: Lost and Found

She was the one who found me, not her husband Helmut.
They were hiking on my mountain;
I had been lying facedown in a ravine
for three thousand years under a glacier,
and when I heard her voice,
my heart, a block of ice,
began to drip within my chest.

At first she didn't recognize me; I was a form under wet glass, and
she thought I was a fellow hiker lost in a storm
and covered in recent snow,
or that I had disappeared within her lifetime,
like the couple lost in 1934
protruding from ice melt,
and stumbled upon by climbers.

"Erika, Ericka," I am thinking, pleading in my frozen inner voice,
"it is me!"
But of course, I speak an ancient language in my head
and my tongue stays motionless,
my lip is pushed up into a sneer,
so how could she possibly hear me?
How *would* she remember me?
And now I hope she will see me though my back is to her,
though I am shrouded in ice,
though so much time has passed.
It is our fate, you know, Erika,
that we be reunited on this mountain.

I was about sixty kilometers from my Feldthurns village,
leading the goats, climbing higher and higher,
sustained on a little grain, some deer meat
you had packed for me.
I was not used to the altitude;
my lungs ached
and my heart felt empty
when an arrow pierced my shoulder.
I don't know who shot it,
a hunter?
I fell.
The snows shrouded me,
at first warming me with a light air blanket,
and then I lost consciousness
and fell into a cold dream.

When I left you
my heart was not warm,
it was preparing itself for a freeze,
something it did many times
and so
I didn't say, "Good-bye, my Erika,
I am leaving now and of course, I will return."
I just turned away again
and left you to fend for yourself.

Cold was easy for me; I was bred for it.
I was told that by generations before me,
through ancient oral history, the
notion that life *must* be cold,
that the snow will always continue
to fall in my blood,
that I cannot go to a warm place.
Glacier is my spirit, the white ghost
of it forever haunts me.

I walked; I was flea-ridden.
I walked; my gut was bloated
with writhing whipworms
living, warm, within me,
eating through me.
I walked; my hip was fractured by wear, though
I was only about forty-five years old.

I was gentle, a tender of animals,
at times as terrified as a sheep or goat
caught between the moon and a shadow,
unable to tell where reality ends or begins.
To fall was welcome,
to freeze was my escape.
No one could melt me.

Now you find me
uncountable years later, and
the rescuers think I am
a modern climber, exposed by the sun.
They dig at me, with my own bow,
rip at my clothes to extricate me,
jackhammer me.
I do not deserve this.

I call silently to you, Erika, I am powerless.
When I am taken and turned to face you,
I look at you with pitiful, frozen eyes
and you know me at last, I think.
You recoil in horror at
my blackened snow-burnt cheek,
my lost nose,
my missing scalp,
my broken, twisted bones.
I am not the man you knew or fed or loved epochs ago.
They shoved me into a coffin to bring me
to civilization, snapping

my twig of an arm
and breaking my spirit.
I wish my heart hadn't numbed to you, Erika,
time and time again.
I wish I hadn't made you brood about me, to imagine
what happened to me all those frozen,
silent times
when my tongue was stuck to my teeth
and my lips were sealed.
I wish I had spoken and embraced you.
If only I had opened my eyes and my mouth when
I chose not to, your breath might have melted me
and I would have been forced to feel.
To see.
To speak to you.
Instead I hid
under the snow
for eons, alone,
waiting for you
to find me
again.

Sandra and Mark, 2006

Stones

He gave her a princess-cut diamond.
She wore it on her left hand.

When she was a child, she learned that
she was a little princess, and she dreamed about
her prince—as girls do:
The prince finds you, he looks upon your face
with adoration, and he falls in love with you.
Takes you, protects you, cares for you.
Forever.

So how did she change into
a slut, a fat whore?
She was his fiancée, his betrothed, his love.
But now she is obese, ugly, worthless,
because he has taught her these truths,
because he reminds her each day
until her crown is crumpled
and she is bent over,
her soul taken by
newts and toads and spells
and witches and
devils.

He used her as a vessel for infection,
he controlled her with fear,
stepped on her soul
and kicked her ego until he had her
cowering in his palm: "You whore, you slut, you bitch."
And he went out with other women:
"Don't ask me where I am,
bitch, I'll go out where and when."

When she was small enough that he couldn't see her,
she packed her broken crown and her royal dreams
in cardboard boxes,
filed a court order of protection,
and fled in her rusty car.

He gave her a princess-cut diamond,
a square, with four sharp corners,
that will soon be sold.
Next time she'll know better.
The ring will have a round stone.

Part 6
New York at the Turn of the Century

For Eve Merriam, Teacher and Mentor

**The Flatiron Building
New York, ca. 1950
Photograph/Jack Margulies**

*Most human beings are driven to seek security and comfort.
But there is another group that can only thrive
on change and the unexpected of New York.*
~Cathleen Nesbit

Soul Food

Illustration/Susan Margulies Kalish

Soul Food

Flushing, Queens.
You are
a glutton's paradise.
Your melting pot of Chinese soup
can fill a Hungarian's emptiness,
or a Colombian's soul.
The dim sum credo:
I believe in turnip cakes, shrimp noodles,
and sticky rice.
Thy steam carts, they comfort me,
they deliver my bowl.
I accept the Tao
of the yin and the yang,
of burning yellow mustard
curled around the fiery chili sauce.
My heart is aflame
and desirous
of the gelatinous,
the crunchy,
the flaky,
the stuffed,
the saucy.
Presented in threes
they are
the holy trinities.

The Lake

Ainsi, toujours poussés vers de nouveaux
rivages,
Dans la nuit eternelle emporté sans retour ...
~from Le Lac, by Lamartine

The day before this day of bright sun,
the water was the broken glass of a Perrier bottle,
a sullen, yet rich green, refractive along the edges,
heavy from the comingling of clouds above.
Now it leans to blue, then gray like the eyes of a
flirtatious fickle female.

On the promenade, a goose approaches,
his broad breast streaked with algae.
At first glance he is made of cracked porcelain
until he plods off to his mate
and honks in her face.
Toward the first bend there is the lull of rushing water
over the storm drain. The grates catch strings of green.
An Asian couple loudly encourages two tiny children
to reach into a plastic bag and retrieve bread crumbs;
these are ritually scattered into the lake, like ashes.
White ducks glide to them.

On the branch of a bush, acting like the bridge of a nose,
a pair of eyeglasses sit
like a disembodied limb;
startling.
Removed from contextual normality,
they become a joke,
they taunt and mock me with blinding reflected light.
Do I dare take them to grab hold of the sun and
focus their thick lenses
on dry leaves?

Children become a photograph etched into a
backdrop of small, shiny, bright yellow flowers in cool green.
Now the lake belongs to Monet.
A woman in her jogging suit bends to brush
her ungainly, brown dog.

At about this time, my heart is pumping,
my hair is weighing heavily on the my neck but pain
flees consciousness.
At the final lap, near the snapping turtles on the rock,
that bake like cakes in the sun,
the trucks on Northern Boulevard no longer exist.
There are only songbirds and geese.
The conversations between water and sky,
the rhythm of feet, and breath, and sweat,
and the vision of the lake, forever moving,
forever the same.

Illustration/Susan Margulies Kalish

Slice of Life

On the Upper West Side.
The *Original* Ray's Famous Pizza
is now $1.75 a slice.
In the next booth,
a heavyset woman with blonde-streaked hair,
baby stroller parked at the table's edge,
sits across from her companion,
a dead man-mummy.
As the woman eats her pizza,
the wizened old face sleeps,
nestled gray, into the collar of a down coat.

K-Joy 98.3 Long Island's Best Music Mix
This report brought to you by Boston Market ...

The woman eats her pizza.
The mummy opens its eyes briefly,
then returns to the dead.

Seems to me you lived your life
Like a candle in the wind ...

The woman eats, the dead returns.
They speak Polish? Russian?
The down coat collar is moved aside,
and a gold earring is revealed.

They are now two women,
with a baby in a stroller,
having an early pizza dinner
on the Upper West Side of Manhattan.

Photograph/Susan Margulies Kalish

On Leaves

She returned in September, not knowing her place
until one day she reclaimed her space on a lofty
height and opened the door and saw
the leaves.

The trees visited the windows, bringing with them
a green canopy.
The tall oaks sighed and bent with breezes
and later, as leaves turned
gold then brown,
children came to the sanctuary, the tree room.
They held their own leaves of white paper
in their small books, blank,
for her to fill. Like hungry birds with mouths agape
they asked to be fed.
They were told that if they forgot to write
their names on their paper leaves,
she would become
an owl and fly out the window,
into the trees and she would say, "Who? Who? Whose leaf is this?"
They laughed easily as the trees grew bare and they traveled
into letters and words and meanings and enigmas.

When snow melted from the branches and
children's heads swelled with ideas,
she wormed in; small buds had began to form on the trees.
The sun strengthened, bursting the buds into
more letters and concepts and pragmatics
and cookies.
She told them about cicadas that were
on their way and how they'd eat the leaves.

One day, a huge dragonfly, bigger than any of them had ever seen,
got trapped between the window panes.

She had no idea how it came to be, but as the faces
lined up at the window and cheered,
"You can do it, Dragonfly!"
to keep up its spirits,
she gently moved each window up, then down,
trying to protect it, in an attempt to free it.
It was trapped and rapidly losing hope
of ever dodging a frog's tongue again at some lake.
She turned her back for a second and at that moment,
one small child, given the gift of wonder,
pulled the lower window down with all her strength,
and lo, the creature was in flight.

It flew away, or so she told them.
It might have dropped to the ground
or have been taken by a breeze.
But it was gone;
the children were not sure how they felt about it,
but they knew they were heroes.

She was taking leave as well.
As the greens and golds and browns and green-again leaves
reflected many seasons of her life,
she imagined herself released
from between the window panes;
she'd find a place where she could live
for a while without movement
and just observe, quietly.
Then, like a trapped dragonfly,
depleted and unable to exercise its gossamer wings,
she would take flight.
Between the changing leaves.

First Med

A walk-in, storefront medical center,
with an overworked, harried staff
looking as white as their uniforms,
is full of those in need.
Usually on weekends.
Long wait.
Tattered magazines.
Radio.
Faces looking back
at faces.

Two chairs in front of a broken window,
roped together with plastic yellow *caution* ribbons,
broken glass outside, in the parking lot.
According to *Ladies' Home Journal*, you can
make this fast and easy dessert …

A woman with a black and blue battered
face and a burned, bandaged hand
sits next to
a man who is reading
and next to
a young, chunky, coughing woman
sucking on her asthma inhaler.
Sitting with her bearded father,
his hand pulling
pork rinds from a bag.
He *couldn't* be from New York.

I- I- I'm fallin' in and out of love with you
I- I- I never loved someone the way I love you …

Older, unkempt, heavyset white woman
followed by a younger black male

158

holding a yellow pad.
He says,
"Sit. Can I get you something?
Coffee?
I can go up to the White Castle."
She says,
"No."
He advances, she retreats.
They sit.
He scratches lists on the yellow pad in two columns.
And there's Nurse Ratchett:
"Here to see the doctor?
Getting a flu shot?"

A nine-year-old boy
sucks on a candy baby bottle nipple
that he inserts into grape powder, then licks.
His father pats his head.
... 95.5 WPLJ
I want to thank you ...
For giving me the best day of my life.

"Are you here to see the doctor?
Getting a flu shot?"
Lose ten pounds by Christmas on
this fast and easy diet.

The receptionist says that
a car spontaneously burst into flames
in the parking lot;
the car next to it caught fire.
Watch out for the broken glass.

Tina, Tina, Proud and Free

Not sure how many men I've been with,
don't know how many men I've known.

I'm thirty-two years old and livin' in the projects.
Got six kids:
Keisha, Darryl, Dwayne, Kenya, Sade, and Shaheim.
And pneumonia.
No money to fill the prescription.
The mayor took me off welfare and my phone don't work,
can't call the worker.
Two kids got shigella, I don't know why,
we clean people, we wash.
It's October and the food's runnin' out.
We can use some soap and detergent.
I don't want to sell my body.

Not sure how many men I've been with,
don't know how many men I've known.

I'm Tina. I'm thirty-two years old. Got six kids.
Why? you askin'.
Because when I was a baby my mother gave me up,
this lady took me in.
She like my mother but she don't love me, not like her own.
So I made my own family, I made my own love,
I made my six kids.
I don't want to sell my body.

I'm thirty-two years old and livin' in the projects.
Got six kids and my food's running low.
Thanks, God bless you for all the boxes.
The clothes and the food.
Look what you did for me. Look in my cabinets.
What you watchin'? My walls move?

See them shimmer and run. They have life, their backs
shine like the moon, they run up and down the walls and into
the cabinets, into my secrets.
Couldn't you help me, call the worker, tell her we hungry?
I don't want to have to sell my body.

Not sure how many men I've been with,
don't know how many men I've known.

I'm Tina. I'm thirty-two years old and I got six kids.
My phone is disconnected, and I can't call
the worker or the supervisor.
They both have hearts with blood that don't move.
Call this number for me.
Thanksgiving is coming.
Thanks for the hams and the turkeys. And the shopping cart. Full.
I am at your door every day and thanking you
for all those collections.
You got any money? Christmas is coming.
I got six kids. They need.
My kid can't play in gym; don't got sneakers.
Please tell the welfare worker.
I don't want to sell my body.

Not sure how many men I've been with,
don't know how many men I've known

I'm Tina. I'm thirty-two years old and I got six kids.
I got green mold growing on all my walls and
my kids is getting sick. Stomachaches.
I'm gonna be a singer. They got a contract waiting for me.
Just got to sign it. No time to get over there.
Not feeling good. My ulcer again.
Or I can do computers. Teach myself.
I'm good with numbers. It's almost March.
Got any money?
I don't want to sell my body.

Not sure how many men I've been with,
don't know how many men I've known.

I'm Tina. I'm thirty-two years old and I got six kids.
They gave me a workfare job. I'm good at the register.
Work for CVS, ringin' stuff up. From four to eleven.
My neighbor watches the kids. Gotta run to work as soon as they
come home from school. When I get home, some are sleeping,
some are waiting for me in the dark, their eyes wide.
No check from welfare to pay the sitter yet.
I worry about the kids when I'm out.
I worry about coming home on the bus when it's
near midnight, the streets empty.
Got any money to help make ends meet? Easter is coming.
I don't want to sell my body.

Not sure how many men I've been with,
don't know how many men I've known.

I'm Tina. I'm thirty-two years old and I got six kids.
It's May, and I need you to call my worker.
Call and tell her you need to know when I'm gonna
get my money.
Talk to her, woman to woman,
mother to mother,
one human to one human.
Tell her you can't help me forever.
That you been callin' for seven months.
That CVS didn't work out.
That I'm gonna try to do it alone.
Get my own job.
Tell her.
It's going on summer.
And
I don't want to sell my body.

9/11 Lamentation

Lamentation
Illustration/Susan Margulies Kalish

Reflections on Broken Glass

1

I saw this, I saw it all:
The reduction, the demise, the hell, the dust,
I know the horror, the collapse, the fall.

From planes aloft, received the call,
The quick *good-byes*, now lives adjust,
I saw this, I saw it all.

The planes slammed, then a fireball,
Turns the rubble to a crust;
I know the horror, the collapse, the fall.

I see the replay, I know the appall,
Weeping is my only must,
I saw this, I saw it all.

In body bags, the short, the tall.
The carcasses of cars now rust,
I know the horror, the collapse, the fall.

The enemy lurks, so brazen, such gall,
I fear the end of time once just,
I saw this, I saw it all,
I know the horror, the collapse, the fall.

2

He jumped, calmly he dropped,
One of six thousand, fifty-five missing people
Head first and disappeared.

The fireball wrought gray dust,
Quartz, sand, glass, souls:
He jumped, calmly he dropped.

What choice was there, oh Lord,
For the thirty or more facing immolation?
Head first and disappeared.

The indelible image, the work clothes,
Dark pants, white shirt, tie,
He jumped, calmly he dropped.

A young doctor opened the body bag
And recoiled at the pieces,
Head first and disappeared.

Forever with me the image,
That vision; sacred life-death moment, when,
He jumped, calmly he dropped,
Head first and disappeared.

What I Heard on the Morning News

A young doctor opened the body bag
and said,
"Oh, my God."
She wasn't prepared for the leg, the pelvis,
the penis,
the raw intestines,
the pants pocket
that once held a wallet,
identification, faces.
A life.
Someone said:
"Another part of him came in earlier,
with his cell phone."

Holding Hands

Women dropped,
holding hands,
in twos,
like they did in the
Triangle Shirtwaist fire of 1911:
but in those days, buildings did not have
one hundred ten floors.

Woof and Warp

Early Saturday morning
light rain
hits the air conditioner
and taps the skylight.
I hear a dog bark,
a bird sing.
It's January
and the world is upside down;
maybe we are really in China,
lying in bed, on pale percale sheets, listening
as 6:00 AM sky patrols
roar overhead,
flying in formation,
leaving double white trails
of crisscrossing, frozen, parallel exhaust
that remain for hours;
some formed woof,
some formed warp
as the sky loomed.

There is need to tighten
the knots and fibers
to mend the holes,
repair the fabric.
But with what?
The old dye-lot has run out,
and a new thread can only be
similar yet different;
it can close a tear
but the weave
forever rent
is illusively contiguous.

Pine Barren

January 2002

In the heart of Manhattan
on a cold Sunday afternoon,
I looked up to a sky
that was blue and cut viciously
by the corner of
a white-brick residential tower.

It was an Edward Hopper moment.
There was the visage,
a window on the top floor,
south corner,
its eye blind
to the sun,
perhaps asleep midday,
the covers pulled over its head,
taking a nap,
having a disorienting
dream.
The kind of dream midday sleep yields.
Or perhaps it was trying to retreat to sleep
and hide from a painful memory.

Above the window,
on the roof was a tree,
a pine,
green but thin,
scraggly from the waist up.
Bent to the north
as far as it could go
without snapping,
away from a horrible wind
blowing up
from Manhattan's
southern desert.

Part 7
The Last Song

The author with her father
Playground 5, Stuyvesant Town, New York City, ca. 1956
Photograph/Pauline Margulies

There's only one corner of the universe you can be certain of
improving, and that's your own self.
~Aldous Huxley

Connecting the Dots

1

Seeing Stars

It was a cold day, maybe in November of 1954,
around my sixth birthday or perhaps not far after,
when my father took me by the hand.
I see my plaid coat; I feel the itchy wool, coarse to my touch.
I see its red and green box design and a hat to match
tied under my chin.
The coat had a brown mouton collar, and the
bonnet had the same fur around the edges.
I don't remember if I knew how to tie the bow
with the strings in my small cold hands.
Did we take the bus? Probably the subway
to the Upper West Side of Manhattan, to
the Hayden Planetarium.
How did my small thin legs
climb so many steps,
make so many transfers between
the east and west sides of the city?
My feet shivered through my red shoes.
My father's hand was warm.
He was taking me to see the stars.

2

John Cameron Swayze

There were many seats in the domed, round, warm auditorium.
A monster—a projector, though I didn't know it then—
sat central like a huge ant, an alien, crafted
by Carl Zeiss,
filled with glass and light;
it would change my life.

The room darkened and all at once the universe brightened
on the ceiling; I was terrified. I was a city child,
I didn't *have* this many stars, I didn't know them or
comprehend them. I was used to the occasional smattering
in the sky, strewn about,
competing with the city lights.

Aside from terror that day, I learned fear and respect.
The lecturer aimed his flashlight arrow at a constellation
in white pointillism, high above us:
Orion.
He connected the dots and the warrior appeared;
he called the three stars in his belt "John, Cameron, Swayze."
Those who knew the name of the newscaster
laughed.

I learned what Sunday School taught
and what I couldn't understand,
that there *was* a God
and that he was bigger
than we could imagine,
comprising points of light, too many to count.
And then the unthinkable happened; the stars began to move
and became indelibly imprinted on my conscious
and my subconscious,
so burned on the inside of my eyelids
that I could never escape them.

I peeked at the swirling expanse from between my fingers
as I would three years later,
when I was alone in the house and watched
Lon Chaney in *The Mummy*.
The fear was too much for me, the movement too fast,
the years were passing,
time was accelerating,
the ceiling was spinning out of control,
throwing me into a pool of universal chaos and disorder.

I was never the same after that. I was becoming Dave in *2001*,
writhing in loss of control as the Milky Way took over,
sucking me in,
swirling me around,
into the vortex.
I was grabbing at time and space;
all dimensions were spun into the mix—
black holes and white stars becoming one gray, rotating,
threatening cloud.
Save me!

Every time I closed my eyes after that day
I saw *the stars*.
They followed me, taunted me, dared me to grow up.
Terrified me.
They would not stop harassing me as they swirled
beneath my eyelids.
For years they were the boogeyman
in the closet, or the monster under the bed.
The stars. The cold pinpricks of white that I would later learn
were suns.

3

Shooting Stars

In 1973, I was propelled into the mountains of Utah
in a car packed with camping equipment.
A tent, gallons of water. A Portosan nearby,
a herd of cows, grazing.
Altitude defied the heat of summer days.
The light faded to a glow on the horizon and
bounced pink and purple off arches and canyons
into the rim of the sky,
which dulled to black velvet;
the projector was turned on again
for the first time in years.
I was abducted, into the place of fear,
of awe, of fright.
The magnificence; the power, the sky—so chaotic yet neatly
sprinkled with white dust—
was beyond a child's grasp,
beyond an adult's comprehension.
The number of points became
Zeno's conundrum, uncountable, indivisible, defining
what could never be defined.
Lying on my back, I prayed;
numbers were my psalms.
I couldn't complete one page in the Bible of science,
of the holy universe.
I kept losing count,
I didn't know the language
of this foreign place—
And there, behold! Light begat light!
A shooting star!
The sky began to rotate.

4

The Black Box

Now *this* painting is branded into me; a secret is revealed to me.
It is the explanation—that *nothing can be explained.*
That it's too much, too vast to understand.
It goes where I go, in the box where I carry
Orion,
John Cameron Swayze,
myself at age six,
my plaid coat and hat,
my youth,
my childhood fears,
Lon Chaney.
My father.
They are all in there somewhere,
swirling like the stars,
wreaking havoc with the universe of my memories,
pummeling me with laser guns, spewing points of light
at my minimal comprehension.
I am awestruck by what I have collected
inside of me;
I take the pencil in my small hand
and try to connect the dots.

I am old now. I have but one more adventure yet to come.
The adventure that comes to all living things.
What does a man leave behind but his name
and the stories he told?
All else is dust.
~Donald Margulies,
from the play
Shipwrecked! An Entertainment—
The Amazing Adventures of Louis de Rougemont
(As Told by Himself)

POETRY

"*She could see to the horizon to where the Brooklyn and Manhattan bridges formed necklaces.*" So writes Susan Margulies Kalish in *The Cerebral Jukebox*, her first collection of poetry. With an astute eye for the telling detail, she evokes her childhood in Manhattan's Lower East Side. Stuyvesant Town, a middle-class housing development of a hundred look-alike buildings, became her mid-city haven during the baby boom that followed World War II.

Her favorite jukebox hits of the Fifties filter through free verse vignettes, recalling a time of innocence, while the songs of the Sixties echo the turbulence of her coming of age in a time of great change. In succeeding sections she celebrates family, travel, and historical connection, bringing the book's jukebox journey full circle.

Complete with the author's illustrations that eloquently weave together family and neighborhood photographs throughout, *The Cerebral Jukebox* shares unforgettable recollections from one woman's life as she matures from childhood to adulthood in the greatest city in the world.

Susan Margulies Kalish is a native New Yorker. She taught deaf and special needs students in the New York City school system for thirty-three years. Now retired, she still lives in New York City with her husband and son. She enjoys writing, blogging, photography, making jewelry, and replaying memories.

U.S. $14.95

ISBN 978-1-4401-7254-0

 iUniverse®
www.iuniverse.com

90000

9 781440 172540